the second nine months

the second nine months

One woman
tells the *real* truth
about becoming
a mom.

Finally.

A MEMOIR

VICKI GLEMBOCKI

Da Capo
LIFE
LONG

A Member of the Perseus Books Group

Versions of sections of this book were previously published in
Women's Health, *Philadelphia Magazine*, and *Fit Pregnancy*.

Designed by Pauline Brown
Set in 11.5 point Bell MT by the Perseus Books Group

First Da Capo Press edition 2008

Glembocki, Vicki.
    The second nine months: one woman tells the real truth about becoming a mom : finally. a memoir / Vicki Glembocki.
        p.   cm.
        ISBN-13: 978-0-7382-1101-5
        ISBN-10: 0-7382-1101-X
        1. Glembocki, Vicki.   2. Mothers—Biography.   3. Motherhood.   I. Title.
        HQ759.G54   2008
        306.874'3—dc22

                                                              2007035605

Published by Da Capo Press
A Member of the Perseus Books Group
www.dacapopress.com

Da Capo Press books are available at special discounts for bulk purchases in the U.S. by corporations, institutions, and other organizations. For more information, please contact the Special Markets Department at the Perseus Books Group, 2300 Chestnut Street, Suite 200, Philadelphia, PA, 19103, or call (800) 255-1514, or e-mail special.markets@perseusbooks.com.

10 9 8 7 6 5 4 3 2 1

For Blair

contents

MONTH 1   shock and awe   1

MONTH 2   a mother's milked   33

MONTH 3   never let them see you mother   65

MONTH 4   i am wrong. i am invisible. i am mother.   97

MONTH 5   see mommy run. run, mommy, run.   127

MONTH 6   mothers of invention   159

MONTH 7   mommy gone wild   183

MONTH 8   hope springs maternal   203

MONTH 9   it's going to suck   223

MONTH 10   because it's really ten months   247

acknowledgments   263

shock and awe

"By month's end, you'll have settled into a
comfortable routine with baby . . . . You'll
also feel like a seasoned pro."

—*What to Expect the First Year*

I have the distant memory of a moment.

I am in the hospital. I am alone. It's just after four
in the morning. I wake up and realize that it's been
five hours since the nurse last brought me my newborn baby for a feeding. I decide that the baby is dead.

I'm supposed to be sleeping. I'm supposed to be
taking advantage of this.

"Let the nurses keep the baby in the nursery at
night," the instructor advised during the Baby Basics
Brunch my husband and I went to in January, when I
was seven months along, armed with two blank note-
books and the expectation that, after the three-hour

seminar, we would know all there was to know about having a baby. She introduced us to the term "mucous plug." She reminded the mothers-to-be, while circling her hand over her pubic bone, that we would need to take extra-special postpartum care of our "swollen girlfriends."

"Should you invite all your friends and family and neighbors and the guy who picks up your trash to drop by the hospital? NOOOOOO!" she yelled, then slammed her hand down on the podium while honking like a game-show buzzer. "Sleeeeeep," she crooned. "You'll need it."

I needed it. I'd been awake for thirty-nine hours straight starting when my water broke, three weeks early, forty-five minutes after my husband left for work, as I was rolling the bison that had traded places with my body out of bed. I chose, then and there, to believe that my water hadn't broken. I chose to believe I'd just peed myself. That was my only option. I was on deadline for an article I was writing for *Philadelphia* magazine, where I work. The story was due on St. Patrick's Day, two days away.

I also hadn't yet packed an overnight bag for the hospital. I hadn't cooked the forty-seven casseroles I'd planned on freezing for Thad and me to eat during my maternity leave. I hadn't shaved my legs. Hanging on my fridge was my "List of Things to Do Before the Baby Comes." "Having the Baby" was not one of them.

Driving myself to the hospital was also not one of them. Nor was having my epidural wear off twice, or flipping off the anesthesiologist at 3:30 in the morning, or roaring at the obstetrician, "Get this thing OUT of me!"

My daughter was now almost fifteen hours old, and I'd not referred to her by the name we'd given her because it just seemed too bizarre, too presumptuous, like this was all some kind of make-believe game and she was some kind of make-believe baby.

"Blair."

Weird.

Every time I tried to say it, I found myself rattling my head back and forth, as if trying to dislocate an embarrassing memory that had seeped into my brain.

But none of that matters now. Because the baby is dead. Why else wouldn't the nurse have brought her in? She just doesn't know how to tell me. If I were the nurse, I'd wait until morning, too. When the patient's rested. When the patient's had a cup of coffee. When the patient's husband is back and able to restrain her. I'd sent Thad home just before midnight, claiming that I wanted at least one of us to get a full night's sleep. But that wasn't true. I wanted to be alone. I needed time by myself to process this change that had just occurred in my life.

Yesterday? No baby.

Today? Baby.

Just as I pick up the phone to dial the nursery, the door squeaks open. The nurse rolls in the baby in her hospital-issued plastic mobile travel system that I decide we should steal. The baby is crying.

"I think she's pretty hungry," the nurse says as she hands me the baby, who seems so impossibly tiny and, at the same time, so impossibly huge. Then she leaves. I stare at the closed door, expecting it to open again, expecting the nurse to come back in, to do something about this crying, to read aloud to me from the manual I've been waiting for someone to drop off in my room. But, no. The nurse is gone. The nurse has left me alone. With a baby.

This is the first time the baby and I have been alone together since she was inside me, back when I thought of her as an abstract organ, an extra appendage that compelled me to eat Cap'n Crunch and pee all the time.

"Hey, kiddo," I whisper in a voice so tender that I'm not sure if it's actually coming out of my mouth.

"It's mommy," I say. This is the first time I've ever called myself "mommy." I tug the receiving blanket away from her mouth and push her blue-and-white-striped knit cap high on her forehead, imagining that, if I clear her view, she might recognize me. Or I might recognize her.

I stare, trying to see behind the red face and the swollen eyes and the grunting cry she's making. And, suddenly, this whoosh of hugeness bubbles up in my chest. I've never felt anything like it before. I can't figure out what it is. Terror? Bliss? I decide it must be bliss. It *has* to be bliss, all warm and thick and pulsing with electricity as it slides up my neck and down my arms. I start to sing the first song that pops into my head: "When the moooooon is in the seventh house, and Jupiterrrrr aligns with Mars. . . . " The baby quiets down. This is a good sign. She latches on to my nipple. Another good sign. I force myself not to think about how freaky it is that there is food secreting from a part of my body and a living thing eating the food that's secreting from a part of my body. Instead, I sing: "Aquariuuuuuuusssss . . ." That's what new moms are supposed to do. Sing. Nurse. Soothe. Sing. Nurse. Soothe.

And I'm doing it. I'm doing it all. And I feel pretty okay that I'm doing it. *I'm going to dig this mommy thing*, I think. This is how I imagined it would be.

• • •

Two weeks later, I push the stroller down a street I've never been on before. This is the first walk the baby and I are taking together. There is probably a line in the baby book my mother gave me, the one that's still in its plastic box in one of the many piles on our dining

room table, where I'm supposed to document this moment—First Walk in Stroller. Taking this walk is
supposed to be relaxing. *The Girlfriend's Guide to Surviving the First Year of Motherhood* said so—"Get out
and get fresh air . . . it does wonders for your spirit."
My spirit is supposed to be inhaling the warm, late-
March air, feeling invigorated while I maternally
point out the many things the baby is seeing for the
first time. The buds on the maple trees. The trail from
an airplane. The tabby cat sunning itself on the back
stoop of the white house we just passed. But I'm not.
Because the baby is crying.

I push faster.

She keeps crying.

I hum "Twinkle, Twinkle, Little Star."

She keeps crying.

I shift the angle of the canopy, in case the sun's
shining in her eyes.

She keeps crying.

I reach down the back of her neck, under the cotton blanket she's swaddled in, under her lavender one-
piece bodysuit with the yellow butterfly on it so I can
finger the tag, in case there's a plastic price-tag holder
sticking out of it. Or an open safety pin. Or a pickax.
There's nothing.

She keeps crying.

No matter what I do, she keeps crying.

What I *should* do is turn the stroller around. I should not be in public. I should go home. But I can't go home. Because, a block away, there is a Laundromat, and in that Laundromat are the quilt from our bed and the afghan from our couch, tumbling in an industrial dryer, a task that was on my "List of Things to Do Before the Baby Comes" because the quilt and afghan—too large for our washer and dryer—had fused with zillions of sharp, blond, burrowing dog hairs, discarded by Levi, our 80-pound Lab, that I was certain would break free, lodge in the baby's throat, and choke her. I need to finish this job. I have two hours between each nursing, so there's time to finish this job. I pat along the sides of the baby's swaddle to make sure her fingers aren't bent the wrong way. I tuck the blanket under her feet, in case her feet are cold.

She keeps crying.

What am I doing wrong?

I pull out my cell phone and dial Thad's office line.

"I can't do this," I say, before he even says "hello."

"What happened?" he asks. I hear the wheels on his office chair roll across the floor and his door close. I tell him about the afghan and the Laundromat and the crying. About how I can't stop the crying.

"Is she hungry?"

"No."

"Is she wet?"

"No."

"Maybe you just tried to do too much, sweetie. Maybe you should just go home," he says in his new mellow tone, the one he's been using in the middle of the night for the past two weeks, every time I nudge him awake and declare that I'm certain the baby is dead.

"She's not dead," he always says, calm and patient, just like he was when I woke him up with the same worry thirteen seconds before.

"How do you know that?" I always ask.

"I know."

"*How* do you know?" And Thad flips the covers onto me, staggers over to the Pack 'n Play at the foot of our bed, and leans over so his cheek is next to Blair's tiny mouth, waiting until he feels a few bursts of warm air.

"She's not dead," he whispers, climbing back into bed. I always lie there for a few seconds. Then I get up and check myself, resting my hand lightly on Blair's chest, swaddled so tight I wonder if the receiving blanket is the only thing holding her fragile body together, until I feel it rise, up and down, up and down.

Now, though, in the light of day, his soothing "everything's okay" tenor makes me clamp my teeth together, as if he didn't just suggest I go home but instead told me to do the very opposite, to suck it up, to finish the damn bedspreads, and then make a meatloaf.

"I can't go home, Thad," I yell. "The bedspreads are in the fucking dryer and I am on the fucking street behind the fucking pizza shop and the baby won't stop fucking crying and I'm losing my fucking mind!"

There's a long pause. I know what Thad's doing. He's calculating the right thing to say, believing that there is a right thing to say, not understanding that nothing he says will be right. Because what he wants to do is solve the problem. But he can't solve the problem. Because the problem is me. Mothers are supposed to be able to stop their babies from crying. Mothers are supposed to know what to do.

I don't know what to do.

Wasn't that whole maternal-instinct thing supposed to stick around after that first night in the hospital? Wasn't some maternal gene supposed to switch on and keep me all stoned on bliss and beaming at this child like she is pure light? Like she is the sun? Like, by having her, my life has finally begun and I am finally complete? Isn't that what everyone says at the end of *A Baby Story*? Isn't that what my mother meant when she told me labor was "wonderful pain"? Because I'm not feeling wonderful. In these two weeks since we left the hospital, my emotional range seems to have collapsed in on itself, trapping me in a hole where I feel only overwhelmed. And frustrated. And afraid.

I'm terrified, really. Terrified that Thad and I have made a horrible, terrible mistake by having this baby.

And I want to tell Thad, explain it to him. But that scares me, too. He won't understand. How could he? He's too busy wondering where his wife went. Where is the woman who was so tickled when the plus sign appeared on the pregnancy test that she immediately wrapped it in blue tissue paper with a red bow and express-mailed it to her parents? Where is the woman who lay beside him in bed every Saturday morning, propped up on pillows, reading aloud from the latest chapter in *Your Pregnancy Week by Week*? Where is the woman he took a photo of less than a month ago as she sat at a card table in the kitchen, carefully hot-gluing little plastic toys to a mirror frame to hang in the baby's room, her sweatshirt pulled up to reveal the expanse of her belly? Where was *she*?

"Am I supposed to take the wet bedspreads out of the dryer?" I shout before Thad has a chance to speak, knowing that I'm getting angry at him to keep myself from getting angry at the baby. "Seriously? Is that what you're telling me to do?"

"Do you want me to come home?" he says. *Oh God, yes.* Yes, I want him to come home. I want him to come home more than anything in the entire world. I want him to rescue me. Actually, I want him to come here, to the street, and pick up the baby, and take her home so I can go back to the Laundromat and finish my job. I know I'll feel better if I can accomplish something, and if it's not stopping the baby from crying, it's washing the bedspread and the afghan. It's getting rid of the dog hair. I need to complete this one task to assure myself that I can do at least one thing right.

Of course, Thad can't come home. He started a new job training pharmaceutical reps less than a month ago and his boss already gave him a week off when Blair was born. Plus, he has a forty-minute commute each way. Plus, by the time he'd get here, the laundry would be done anyway.

"I'm fine," I say.

"Are you sure?" Thad asks.

"Yes, I'm fine," I say, again, as if saying it again might make it true. "Just come home as soon as you can." I flip the phone closed.

Just then, the train whisks by above the bushes where the street dead-ends. It's the train I took every morning to get to work. Eighteen minutes from the Westmont station in New Jersey, over the Ben Franklin Bridge, to Center City, Philadelphia. I listen to it pass, the hum of the rails on the track rising in pitch as it picks up speed.

"I wish I was on that train," I say, out loud. A Ford Explorer drives by, the driver watching me talking to myself as I stand next to a vacant lot with a baby stroller and gaze longingly at the train track. He probably thinks I've escaped from an asylum with all this stringy brown hair clumped in a nest on the top of my head, my body hidden in extra-large yellow sweatpants, Thad's blue-and-gray checkered flannel that I've not taken off for four days, and a pair of light blue sandals that I bought at Target the day after I came home from the hospital because my feet had swelled two sizes from the fluids they pumped into me for the epidural that wore off ten minutes before Blair came screaming out of my body.

And, now, she's still screaming. I grab the pacifier out of the stroller's cup holder, the same pacifier the baby has refused to even drool on for the past fourteen days of her life and that I've been carrying around like a talisman, praying on it, *please, for the love of God, just put this thing in your mouth for five minutes, just shut up for five minutes.* She lets the pacifier rest on her tongue, opening her mouth wider to scream around it. I pick her up, and she cries even harder, shrieking almost, as if there could be nothing more upsetting to her than being held by me.

I feel tears running down my cheeks, though they don't feel like my tears and they don't feel like my cheeks. I look at the clock on my phone—there are seventeen minutes left on the dryer cycle, which means I have seventeen more minutes to kill. I slide Blair back in the stroller and start pushing again. I make a right down another street, past a cute house on the corner with a sign in the front yard that reads "Welcome to the Nut House."

I wish I were on that train.

•   •   •

"How much is she eating?" Dr. Weidner asks, seconds after walking into the exam room on Friday to find me there nursing Blair. He's looking kind of embarrassed that he found me nursing Blair, even though it's happened every time we've been to his office so far. And we've been to the pediatrician a lot in the three weeks since she was born.

Blair hadn't been gaining enough weight. She needed to gain weight; she needed to eat more because the more she ate, the faster the bilirubin would flush out of her bloodstream. I didn't know exactly what bilirubin was, only that she had too much of it and that it made her tiny body all yellow with jaundice and sent us to the hospital every morning during the first two weeks of her life to have blood taken from her teeny-tiny heels, leaving them dotted with red, pimply scabs. Every three days, we'd go to the doctor's office for test results and a weight check. All had been going okay. She'd been gaining. Slowly. But gaining.

Until today.

Today, when I carried her naked body to the scale in the hall, the nurse made a tsk-ing sound. Blair had lost 1.5 ounces, an alarming amount when a baby weighs only 6 pounds.

Something is wrong.

"I don't know how much she's eating," I say to Dr. Weidner, looking down at the floor. This is my job.

I'm supposed to know these things now. I'm at least supposed to be able to nourish this child; my boobs are at least supposed to produce enough milk for her. "I don't know how I'm supposed to know how much she's eating."

"Hmmmm," Dr. Weidner replies, his tall, lanky frame looming above Blair as he pokes at her stomach on the exam table, peering through his wire-rimmed glasses as if half-expecting letters to bubble up, *Exorcist*-like, under her skin: *"Help me."*

I glance at the ceiling, scanning for a magic breast milk calculator up there that will spit out a number. How *much* is she eating? Compared to whom? Compared to Thad? Compared to the dog? Compared to the other three-week-old babies I'd spent time with in all my thirty-three years, which is a grand total of zero? I don't know how much she's eating because she is eating from my *boobs!* She is sucking milk *out of my boobs!* Or I *think* she's sucking milk out of them, at some point after the hour it takes me to convince her to even latch on, which has been our routine ever since we left the hospital and she apparently decided that my boobs were covered in Mad Dog and, thus, should be avoided at all costs. Now, instead of latching, she wails, while I frantically try and position myself for nursing, piling throw pillows under my arms, then pulling them away, then lying down on my side, then sitting up, then tilting her head a few degrees one way, then the other, then stopping, then crying myself for a few minutes.

Why is this so hard for me?, I wonder. *Why can't I do this one simple thing that women have been doing for bazillions of years?* Then, when I notice her mouth is open huge, mid-wail, I'll grab the back of her head and squash her mouth into my breast as if the pressure alone might suction hΔer on. But even once she's there, how would I begin to determine how much she's eating? Do I weigh my boobs? Before and after? Can I do that? Is there a special scale? Do they sell them at Babies "R" Us? Would I have to remove my nursing bra to use it, because it took me twenty-eight minutes to figure out how to put it on, and I'm never taking it off again. Ever.

"Ohhhh . . ." I say, because I have to say something to the doctor. "She eats every two hours. More or less twelve times a day. Anywhere from fifteen minutes to an hour at a time."

"No formula?"

"No formula."

"Hmmmmmm." I envision what Dr. Weidner is writing in that manila folder of his: *Mother inadequate. Bad boobs.*

"Besides the weight, everything looks okay with *her,*" Dr. Weidner says, though I'm not sure he really emphasized the word. "Do you still have that supplemental nurser?"

I stare at Dr. Weidner's face. He raises his eyebrows, his way of asking the question again without verbally asking it. But I can't answer him. I just stare, as if he's just asked if I still have the placenta. As if he expects me to pull a Ziploc out of my diaper bag and hand it to him. *Why yes, doctor, I have that placenta right here . . .*

I still have the supplemental nurser. A lactation consultant gave it to me while we were at the hospital. Not every nursing mom gets one, but not every nursing mom has a baby with jaundice. The nurser, she explained, would add some formula to my breast milk to ensure that Blair got more food, enough to wash out the bilirubin. If we supplemented with a bottle instead, the baby might develop "nipple confusion," she explained, dropping her voice forbiddingly, as if the only thing that could be worse for a newborn would be bubonic plague. So every two hours, every time Blair needed to eat, every time she stuck out her tongue and puckered her mouth and cried that desperate, bleating, inconsolable cry that made me question, again and again, if she was human, I would first heat up a 5-ounce bottle of formula. Then I'd screw the bottle, upside down, into the supplemental nurser—a holder with a tube attached to it that clipped to the strap of my nursing bra. I'd tape the tube to my breast, careful to make sure that the end of the tube was perfectly aligned with the tip of my nipple, which usually took about seven tries. Then began the hour-long latching ritual, while also making sure that the tiny end of the skinniest tube in the known universe was in Blair's mouth so, when she sucked, she got both my breast milk and the formula.

I hate the supplemental nurser. Not because it leaks. Not because it keeps plugging up with air bubbles, which means I have to take it apart, rinse it out, and start over again. Not because I am the only one who can tape it on and coax Blair to use it, every two hours, twenty-four hours a day.

I hate it because it reminds me, every time, that I am failing at this mommy thing. That this poor child has been cosmically paired with the only woman in the world who doesn't have any maternal DNA, who doesn't instinctually know what to do with a baby, whose body parts don't even function the way a woman's are designed to when she has a baby, who can't stop her baby from crying, who couldn't keep her baby from starving, who can't look at her baby and feel anything but dread.

Especially now. Because everyone has gone. My in-laws drove the four hours home to central Pennsylvania the day we were discharged from the hospital. My parents left two days later, driving three hours farther, all the way across the state. Thad's gone back to work.

And now it's just me. And Blair. And the supplemental nurser.

Everything depends on me. It's all up to me.

Which is why I was so relieved on Monday, three days ago, after the bilirubin levels had gone down and the weight had jumped up, when Dr. Weidner told me I could stop supplementing. I actually considered kissing him. Blair and I could be *normal* now and nurse the *normal* way, the way all moms did. As soon as we got home, I plopped down on the couch with her. I unbuttoned my shirt, then coaxed her on, without really even having to coax her, without turning on the TV like I always did, hunting for a Lifetime movie that would numb my brain enough to keep me from dwelling on how much I hated this. This time, for the first time, it was just me.

I relaxed. I decided Blair relaxed, too. We locked eyes. We *looked* at each other. And, just for a second, I sensed the anxiety that had been suffocating me since Blair was born lift off me. And finally I felt capable, adequate. I felt like a mother is supposed to feel. Blissful, even. And I'd felt that way, on and off, for the past three days.

Until today.

"Yes," I say to Dr. Weidner. "I still have the supplemental nurser." I swallow hard. Suddenly, all the joy is gone. Suddenly, I'm right back where I started except, now, I'm even more worried about her weight.

"Oh, Blair," I say, laying her down on the examining table so my back is to the doctor, retucking her swaddle so it looks like I have a reason to turn away. She starts to cry. "I told you to stay away from that Billy Rubin. I told you he was bad news."

"Bilirubin . . . that's funny," Dr. Weidner says, laughing freely like a man who can leave this room and not even have to *think* about Blair until our next appointment, a week away. Seven days away. One-hundred-and-sixty-eight hours away. Eighty-four feedings with the supplemental nurser away. "It's great that you have a sense of humor about all this."

When I get home, I let the dog out and leave him in the backyard while I look for the supplemental nurser, clawing though drawers in Blair's room, through the closet, as if this is Thad's workshop in the basement, not the bedroom we painstakingly painted two shades of purple before finding the perfect color that contrasted the red crib sheet and matched the rainbow-striped valances and dust ruffle my mother had made. I find the nurser on a shelf, under the stack of burp cloths. I carry Blair to the family room and sit down on the couch, belting the My Brest Friend nursing pillow around my waist, so stiff that it sticks out in front of my stomach like a shelf. I turn on the television. I unbutton Thad's flannel shirt, which I'm wearing again, and unsnap both cups of my nursing bra so both my boobs hang out. I hook up the nurser. It's upside-down, attached to my left bra strap. I tape the end to my nipple, then snake the tube over my very full, rock-hard boob while the other sticks straight out like a missile. The baby is half on the pillow, half in my arms. After nearly forty-five minutes of false starts and screaming, she latches on.

Then I hear the dog bark.

He is barking as if four men carrying sickles have just scaled the fence and are circling him. I suspect he is barking at my neighbor, my new neighbor, who decided to start building a house on the empty lot next to ours five days after Blair was born. Over the past week, the contractor—whom Thad nicknamed Pompadour—has been ringing my doorbell at least two times a day. *Can you move your minivan? Can the concrete guys use your driveway? Can they stand on your garage?* Pompadour doesn't seem to comprehend that this is not a community project. That I don't care. And, now, here he is. Again. This time, at the back gate.

The dog is distracting me. He is distracting the baby. He must be stopped.

I stand.

I walk to the sliding glass door.

I drag open the door.

I step out onto the deck.

I glare down at the man standing at the gate.

"What the hell do you want from me?" I scream.

"Can you . . . um . . . can you call your dog?" the man asks, looking at the dog, at the sky, at the ground, anywhere but at me. "We need to get the branch."

It is only then that I realize that the man standing at the gate is not Pompadour. The man is from a tree-cutting service hired, I presume, by the couple who lives behind us to remove the enormous tree branch that fell into our yard during the windstorm two nights ago. I look out into the yard. Yes, the branch is there. Also there are three other men from the tree-cutting service, staring up at me. And My Brest Friend. And my baby. And my boobs.

●　　　●　　　●

I shimmy one of the baby books out of the pile stacked on the family room floor and thumb through the index. *Bath. Bathing.* I grab another one. *Bathing: newborn.* And another. *Bath: fear of.*

In the past three weeks, I've spent $122.75 on baby books—adding to the hundreds I'd spent stockpiling them during the first nine months—ordering from Amazon every time a friend called or e-mailed to check on how we were doing, always recommending a book that she couldn't live without or that her sister swore by or that she saw on the *Today* show.

"Send Thad out to buy *The Happiest Baby on the Block* immediately," Rebecca instructed.

"*The No-Cry Sleep Solution*," Jenn wrote. "Get this NOW."

And I did. *The Baby Book. The Girlfriend's Guide to Surviving the First Year of Motherhood. The Womanly Art of Breastfeeding. Your Baby and Child. Healthy Sleep Habits, Happy Child.*

I keep them as close to me as I possibly can, always within reach, this little book-fortress on the floor next to the couch that I've decided will surely protect me—and Blair—from everything I don't know.

"The first bath is very scary," my mother warned last night on the phone when I told her that Blair's weird, black, belly-button scabby thing had fallen off so she could finally take a bath—a good thing, since her fuzzy tonsure of brown hair was so greasy, Thad had started calling her Pony Boy.

"Why is it scary?"

"It just is. The baby's so slippery," she explained. "You know, Aunt Mamie always came over to help give the first bath, just so someone who knew what to do would be there."

"Mom, Aunt Mamie can't help me," I said. "Aunt Mamie is dead."

After flipping through nine books, I settle on *What to Expect the First Year.* It lays out the process step-by-step (3. "Run water." 4. "Undress baby completely.") and also offers accompanying illustrations. Illustrations are good. Illustrations make it impossible for me to screw this up. I instruct Thad to read through each step, then dispatch him to the bathroom to prepare, yelling out reminders in his wake. *Remember, you need two washcloths. Remember, you need cotton balls to clean her eyes. Remember, you need water.*

I'm glad our friend Julie is here. She drove in last Thursday from Penn State, where all of us met each other years and years ago. Thad and I both knew Julie before we knew each other. She managed the bar that was connected to the restaurant where I worked when I was in college. Every time she saw me back then, she would hand me a drink that she'd created especially for me, called Rum Punch, which she never made me pay for. Julie was my go-to person—the person who hooked me up with her mechanic buddy Bob when my '73 baby-blue Volkswagen bug started stalling at red lights, the person who scored a white limo to drive us to Bucknell to see an Indigo Girls concert, the person who let me live with her years later when I moved back to town to write for the alumni magazine. I cleaned her house in exchange for rent, let her try to teach me how to throw a football, and hung out with her while she was bartending—which is when I met Thad, late on a Friday night near the stage where a metal cover band was playing "Back in Black." I thought he was hot—this guy drinking the Amstel with the wavy dirty-blond hair and the muscular forearms and the chiseled cheekbones and the posture of a person who had to be comfortable in his own skin, to know exactly who he was. Without asking if I needed another drink, he bought me a 7&7. Then I asked him a question that he says made him fall for me: "What do you want to be doing in five years?"

As it turned out, a little over five years later, we were engaged. Julie was the "best man" in our wedding two years ago. We've always called her Mac-Gyver because she can fix anything, and I was hoping, secretly, that when she came to meet Blair, she would figure out some way to fix me.

She arrived at our front door armed with her softest sweatshirt, which she claimed all babies loved to snuggle against. She also claimed all babies loved her, which appeared to be true. Minutes after she arrived and held out her arms, Blair, who was swaddled up tight in a pink gingham receiving blanket, gazed up at Julie as if she hadn't been crying nonstop since long before the sun had come up that morning. As if she hadn't been crying longer and more frequently every day since the Laundromat incident. As if she were, in fact, a sweet and contented bundle of joy.

"She looks like you," Julie said, as she sat down on the couch with Blair in her arms.

"What're you talking about?" I asked, only half-listening as I rushed around the kitchen, energized by the presence of another grownup, someone *else* who could hold the baby and give me a few untethered minutes to get some order in my life, to put the cereal bowls in the dishwasher, run the garbage disposal to get rid of that sour smell wafting from the sink, spray the countertop with Fantastik so I could scrub off the drips of coffee and yogurt and formula that would, normally, never have been there when company was coming over. I also wouldn't normally have had 2-inch-deep purplish-black circles under my eyes or be dressed in a yellow shirt, a color that makes me look like a corpse. But it had buttons down the front, which was pretty much the only requirement of my life these days since it allowed me the luxury of whipping out a boob and attaching the nurser to it without revealing the bulge that was my stomach, which still looked about six months pregnant, except now it wasn't hard with baby. Now it was wiggly and jiggly and pocked with fat.

"She has your eyes," Julie said.

"She does not. They're Thad's eyes. See how light blue they are?"

"I don't know, Vicki. They look like your eyes to me. They might be Thad's color, but they are your shape. And that's your nose."

"You think?" I asked, as I sidled up next to Julie on the couch. We both stared at Blair's tiny round face. She wasn't looking at anything in particular, her lids almost translucent with those long black eyelashes brushing the tops of her cheeks each time she blinked, her bottom lip pouting out just like Thad's does. My mother called it her "Daddy Lip." My mother thought she looked like Thad. Everyone thought she looked like Thad. I wanted her to look like me.

I thought she looked like me, in the first week, when I was still popping Percocet, when Thad and I were still fueled on adrenaline, telling everyone who called how lucky we were because Blair was sleeping so much. Once our parents left, once Thad and I were alone with Blair for those few idyllic days before he went back to work, we flew out of bed in the morning, each of us vying to get to Blair first, to be the first to hold her, to be the first to change her diaper. We spent the rest of the day sitting on the couch, cuddled together like a real-life family, Blair sleeping, swaddled like a burrito, lying in the crook of Thad's arm.

Thad looked like he was made to have a baby in his arms, or on his chest, warm under the red cotton blanket that had the least amount of dog hair on it, Blair's head sticking out just far enough that Thad barely had to lean forward to kiss the top, which he did approximately every eight seconds. I imagined this was how it would be—how he would be—years ago, when we brought the tan, 5-pound puppy home from the SPCA and Thad spent every night for a week sleeping with him on the kitchen floor that we'd carpeted in thirty-seven layers of the *Centre Daily Times*. We weren't married yet or even engaged, just living together near Penn State, renting a farmhouse

on the side of Nittany Mountain, talking about getting married, maybe, while we gushed over Levi's
sweet puppy breath.

"If we feel this gooey about Levi, can you imagine
how we'd feel about a baby?" I asked Thad, again and
again, though I suspect I kept repeating it so I could
hear it myself, so I could remind myself that I actually
had the capacity to feel this kind of gooiness over
something. As an only child, I'd always pretty much
believed the world revolved around me. My parents,
who'd spent nine years desperately trying to conceive,
considered a baby a miracle. Then I had the good for-
tune of being the only grandchild within a three-state
radius, my grandmother rarely dropping by without
first stopping at the Super Duper to buy me a cupcake.
My mother came to every performance of every play I
was in. My father never raised his voice at me—not
once—and the only time I can remember his being in
any way upset was when I started choking on a piece
of spinach at Elby's Big Boy and he flipped me upside
down, held my feet, and shook me. That is what I
knew. I was accustomed to being the recipient of gooiness. So this dog-thing felt strange, as if the existence
of Levi had triggered a part of my brain that had
never before synapsed.

Even stranger, though, was my reaction to Thad's
reaction to the dog. Because for every ounce of gooiness I displayed, Thad expressed a 5-gallon drum. He

was gooey with gooiness, rolling around with Levi in the grass, goading Levi to lick the entire surface of his face, taking hundreds of photos of Levi just standing, just sitting, just sleeping on his newspaper bed. Watching Thad's gooiness over the dog made me feel gooier over Thad, made me more certain that this man truly was kind. And nurturing. And fun. That this man was real—a bona fide "good guy." A keeper.

And watching Thad with Blair? Watching him tuck her inside his fleece so she could lie on his bare chest for what he called "heartbeat therapy"? It's no wonder I confided in my friend Sabrina during our first week home with Blair that I never realized I could love Thad as much as I did then, as he and I overflowed with revelations about this beautiful, marvelous creature, about how blessed we were to have her in our lives. And we took inventory. Her seashell ears were Thad's. Her hairline, Thad's. Her fair skin, Thad's. Her mouth, Thad's. Her eye color, Thad's. Her eyes, mine. Thad couldn't see it, so I grabbed my baby book and showed him my newborn pictures. *See the space between the eyes, see the almond shape, see the ducts in the corners. See.*

As I sat on the couch with Julie, seeing Blair through Julie's eyes, it occurred to me that I hadn't really looked at her since that first week—not that I didn't look at her every hour of every minute of every day. But I hadn't looked at her face as deliberately as I

was now. And, now, when I looked, I thought she re-
sembled an alien. So skinny. Her eyes so bulgy and
puffy and blank, poking frog-like out of her shiny bald
head, her face wrinkled up as if she was in some kind
of pain. I couldn't say that out loud—not even to Julie,
who had been one of my closest friends for more
than twelve years. How could I admit that? What
mother sees her baby that way? Julie would think I
was crazy. *Anyone* would think I was crazy. I probably *was* crazy. No one could know that. I had to pretend, to act like everything was okay. *I'm fine. Blair's
fine. We're fine.*

"Jules, you know, I just can't even explain how
much I love her. I can't even fathom it," I said instead.
And Julie smiled, nodding as if to say, *Of course you do.
Of course you love her.*

Now, two days into Julie's visit, as Thad runs water into the bright blue baby tub, I give Julie her as-
signment—the video camera. We'd been neglecting
our parental duty with the video camera since we
came home from the hospital and let Thad's father do
the taping. That meant nine close-ups of Levi, an extended shot—totaling about a half hour or so—of
Thad's mother holding a sleeping Blair with no one
saying a word, and another extensive study of the
pink "It's a Girl" balloon, bobbing in the cool March
wind, tied to the front railing of our yellow bungalow
with the towering maple tree and the dogwood along

the driveway and the azaleas lining the front porch, all getting ready to bloom. Ever since, the camera had been sitting on the kitchen counter next to the stove, plugged in and charged. I looked at it hourly, feeling huge pressure each time, certain that, at any moment, Blair was going to spout off the Preamble to the Constitution and I was going to forget to tape it. And, before we'd know it, she'd be in college and the only thing we'd have on film is our child wrapped in a hospital blanket, wearing the tassel hat my grandmother knitted for her and being sniffed by a dog. So we weren't just going to videotape Blair's first bath. No, this was going to be epic. This was going to be the *Ben-Hur* of baby videos.

"Julie, you need to stand in the tub."

"What?"

"You need to stand in the tub so you can get a direct shot, straight down. See what I'm saying?" I say, as we all kneel on the bathroom floor and I trace an imaginary line in the air from where Julie should hold the camera, just under the shower nozzle, to the spot where Blair will be lying. I'd already swaddled Blair in a yellow receiving blanket because one of my mother's friends told me to do that—immersing a baby in the bath for the first time all wrapped and cozy, she promised, would make said baby love baths forever and always. And since I am desperate for a sign that Blair loves something in her life—anything, really—I follow the advice.

And it works.

I place her in the water all wrapped up and she just gazes straight ahead, her big blue eyes wide, like buttons.

"Is this what it felt like inside mommy?" I ask her, as if she might answer, though I'm really just trying to have some kind of narration on the video. Thad isn't speaking. Julie isn't speaking. So I have to say something. I have to be funny. I have to perform. This video is permanent. You only get one shot to record the first bath.

"I'm ready for my close-up, Mr. DeMille," I say, signaling Julie to pan in while I untuck the swaddle. The transition is instantaneous—from calm, frozen, staring baby to screeching-like-she-caught-on-fire baby, swallowing her breath, her arms and legs flailing, farts exploding out of her bum. I turn to the camera.

"I think we can safely assume she hates the bath," I say. I wink very theatrically. And Thad and I proceed to forget everything we read in the instructions, washing her hair and digging out the cheese curdles trapped in the creases in her armpits, trying not to look frantic, though I'm feeling frantic. Because now it's on record—how bad I am. How unhappy my baby is. This is fast becoming the longest ten minutes of my life, as Blair's cries escalate, passing the barrier of sound so that there is just an open, trembling mouth over a withered naked body that has turned bright red as if we'd poured the bathwater right out of a whistling teakettle.

"Oh, mommy, I hate you so much," I say, in that high-pitched voice Thad and I have used for years when we're speaking for Levi and have both recently appropriated as "Blair's Voice." "I'm only seventeen days old and I hate you." Thad is shushing Blair, just like it said to do in *The Happiest Baby on the Block*. It isn't working. I start to sing.

"I'm going to wash that man right out of my hair. I'm going to wash that man right out of my hair. I'm going to wash that man right out of my hair, and send him on his way."

a mother's milked

"With his small head pillowed against
your breast and your milk warming his
insides, your baby knows a special closeness
to you . . . he is learning about love."

—*The Womanly Art of Breastfeeding*

When I place the very naked, very squirming Blair on
the scale at the pediatrician this morning, her skinny
chicken legs pumping in and out like pistons, she
clocks in at 6 pounds, 14 ounces—her birth weight.

"Finally," I say, feeling my shoulder muscles slacken
and practically melt down my back. The nurse smiles.

She and Dr. Weidner are the only medical profes-
sionals I've been in contact with since the day my
body exploded and a baby flew forth. They are the ones
who've been monitoring the questionnaires I've been
filling out at each well-baby visit, the ones that screen
for postpartum depression. Every appointment, I

expect one of them to sit me down to tell me that I need some help. But they never do. And I wish they would. I wish I had postpartum. Postpartum would be a very acceptable explanation for why I'm feeling the way I am.

"You're fine," the nurse assures me when we're back in the exam room, as I rewrap the tiny newborn diaper around Blair's bum. "Your responses are perfectly normal." Perfectly normal? Maybe my responses on the questionnaire have been perfectly normal. That "quite often" I have felt "sad and miserable." That I have "never" thought about "harming myself." That "not very often" have I "blamed myself unnecessarily when things went wrong," noting in the margin that the blaming has been, in fact, quite justified. But they are asking the wrong questions. For example, is it "perfectly normal" to consider leaving your five-week-old in the car, with the air conditioning on and a Dan Zanes disc in the CD player, and go inside alone to watch *Ellen?* Is it perfectly normal to feel pissed when she won't stop crying long enough for you to take a shower without having to kick your soaking-wet hamhock-of-a-leg out of the shower stall every two minutes to jiggle the bouncy seat she's lying in on the floor next to the toilet? Is it perfectly normal to look down at her while she's nursing and, instead of thinking about how beautiful she is, to think that she's a parasite hanging off your boob?

"Really?" I ask the nurse, hoping she'll look back down at the chart and notice that she calculated the number incorrectly, that my score is higher than any she has ever seen in her entire career.

"Really," she says. "You're fine."

"I haven't slept in four days," I say, forcing myself to laugh, like this is funny. "That's not fine."

"No, but it's normal," the nurse says.

"And she cries all the time," I say, looking down at Blair, whom I'm bouncing up and down on my knees, because she's wailing, and we've found that bouncing occasionally makes her cease and desist for a minute or two.

"Babies cry. That's perfectly normal," she says.

"But she cries a *lot*," I say. It started three weeks ago, around Easter. Something happened, like Blair woke up to the world, like she realized she wasn't going back inside me where it was dark and warm, like she came to terms with the fact that she was going to have to stay here. With us. With *me*. And she started to cry and hasn't really stopped. And, as of two days ago, tears started to accompany those wails—big, round, wet tears that leave salty white trails of evidence down her cheeks.

"Do you think she could have colic?" I ask the nurse.

"You should talk to the doctor about that," the nurse answers, quick and dismissive, as if I just suggested that Blair's newly exposed bellybutton might have developed gangrene.

"I've been wondering if she might have colic," I say to Dr. Weidner as soon as he opens the door. Blair is still crying. My quad muscles are burning so hot from the bouncing I wonder if they might have started to glow. I'd already read the sections on "colic" in my eleven baby books. I started out looking on the "c"-page for "crying," specifically for "crying enough to make one want to put one's baby in one's closet." I read in book after book that if crying lasted more than three hours in a row for more than three days in a row for more than three weeks in a row, it was probably colic, though there was no consensus on what colic was, exactly. *The Girlfriend's Guide* claimed that colic "lies in a baby's tummy," so I poured gas-relief drops into Blair's mouth before each feeding last week. The gas drops didn't help, so I pulled out *The Baby Book*, which stated that Blair's biorhythm may be "upset." I didn't understand what that meant, so I switched to *Your Baby and Child*, where Penelope Leach declared that colic could only be cured by rearranging your life to comfort or hold or bounce your baby, constantly, until those colicky episodes ended.

Except that Blair's colicky episodes, if that's what they were, didn't seem to end. So, according to Penelope Leach, I was supposed to do nothing but hold her for the rest of my entire life. Because that was how I saw my life now—me breastfeeding *this* crying infant on *this* couch in *this* light blue nursing tank with *this* supplemental nurser, forever. Even though, intellectually, I knew better. Even though I was well aware that babies eventually slept through the night, that babies got larger, that babies started walking and talking and eating macaroni and cheese. But I couldn't imagine it happening with Blair. I didn't have any frame of reference. All I knew was that babies didn't sleep, that babies cried. All I knew was that nothing had changed in the past month. Every day seemed exactly the same as the day before. And those days felt like weeks, like time was moving in slow motion. Or had stopped completely.

I wanted to kill Penelope Leach.

What I need right now is confirmation. I need Dr. Weidner to say, "Yes, this is most certainly colic." I need a word. I need a term to use to clarify to my mother and my husband and myself what has been going on with this child since Easter so that I have an explanation besides "She is frequently miserable and appears to hate me."

"I don't know if it's colic, necessarily," Dr. Weidner says. I want to kill Dr. Weidner. But not as much as I want to kill him three minutes later, when he suggests we switch to soy formula in case Blair is crying because she's reacting to the formula. I appreciate that

Dr. Weidner is taking this crying thing seriously and suggesting a solution. What makes me angry is the formula part. Because switching formula means that I will still be using formula, which means that, even though Blair has finally regained her birth weight, I will still need to use the supplemental nurser.

From the doctor's office, I drive directly to Babies "R" Us. Thad and I have been to Babies "R" Us approximately four times every weekend since Blair was born, but this is the first time Blair and I have come alone. I decide we will be able to make it without incident. Soy formula and out.

As we roll up to the door, I find myself thinking a strange thought: *This has been a good day.* Yes, I still have to use the supplemental nurser and, yes, that sucks. But Blair gained weight. The doctor suggested a crying solution. I made the bed. *This has been a good day.* On a day like today, someone in Babies "R" Us will surely peer into the cart and say, "Oh, what a beautiful baby. So quiet. So content." And she will think, *What a good mom that woman must be.*

As soon as the automatic doors close behind us, Blair starts to scream. The cries should sound familiar to me, but they don't because they are ricocheting off the three-story-high ceilings, echoing down the aisles, filling up Babies "R" Us like a sonic boom. People start turning around.

I bounce the cart up and down while inching toward the formula, because we need the formula and I can't just leave, because *this is my life now.* As we pass the stroller department, I hear the voice of an older woman say, "Why doesn't she just give that child a binkie?" I begin to jog. I remember the mass of maxi pad that's taped between my legs to catch the blood and yuck that's still leaking from my body. I feel it shift. I feel it poke out of the right leg-hole of the enormous mesh underwear the maternity ward nurse sent home with me, threatening to break free, to slide down the right leg of my black XL sweatpants and land in a clump of gross on the white tile floor. I do not care. I grab the formula—four bottles of the pre-prepared stuff that costs twice as much as the powder and is way more than we need but I don't care about that either, because hell knows we are not going to be trying this shopping thing again any time soon.

"Hang in there, kiddo," I say to Blair, as we cut our path to the front of the store. "We can do this." Except, when we get to the register, I realize I don't want to do this. What I want is to walk out of Babies "R" Us and leave Blair there, wailing, the V-shaped blue vein popping out of her forehead. Nice people work at Babies "R" Us. Surely someone will take her home and care for her and buy her pretty things. I look at the door and picture myself walking through it, into the parking lot, into the minivan, into my life as it was before, where I was a confident, able, reliable person. Where I laughed at myself. Where I never, ever felt the urge to run away from anything simply because it was hard. I feel my hands letting go of the bar on the cart, my body turning away, my right foot lifting.

"Is your baby okay?" asks the woman working the register, her green smock carefully pressed. She looks like a grandmother. She probably is a grandmother, brimming with that grandmotherly concern I'd have access to every day if I didn't live 500 miles from my entire family.

"Yeah, she's just colicky," I say, because it's easier to just say she has colic. Plus, it feels good to say it, to state something definitively, even if it's not true. I nod and give Grandma Green Smock that look, that head-tilt-eyebrows-up look I make so often I wonder if my face might freeze that way, in a permanent expression of "We're fine. We're really fine."

"Is she wet?" Green Smock asks.

"No," I answer, assuming that she just must have missed my "look." "She has trouble calming herself." The voice in my head keeps yapping: *You're making Blair this way, Vicki. It's your fault. All this anguish you're feeling is rubbing off on Blair. She's mimicking you. She's feeling this way because YOU are.*

"Is she hungry?"

"Um . . . no," I stutter, surprised by the acid in my tone. Green Smock is surprised, too. She looks at me quizzically, then leans over the counter so she can get a better look at Blair, at the crinkled, diaper-rash-red face that's spouting those yelps. Green Smock glares up at me as if, when she looked in, she caught me pinching Blair in the arm. With pliers.

"Are you *sure* she's not hungry?" she asks. What is *wrong* with this woman? Does she want me to climb over the display of 50-percent-off infant sunblock and smack her? Isn't she *trained?* Doesn't she see hundreds of babies every day?

"She. Is. Not. Hungry." I just nursed her, in fact. In the parking lot. In the minivan. In the backseat, strategically positioning myself behind the roller shades we'd fastened to the windows, NPR playing extra loud on the radio—my only contact with the real world in more than a month.

Green Smock from Hell shakes her head, then tells me to swipe my card. As I'm trying my hardest to shoot daggers out of my eyes and through Green Smock's smock, I realize Green Smock *does* see hundreds of babies every day. She *is* trained. If anyone would recognize a deficient mother, a grandmother who works at Babies "R" Us would. Green Smock sees it. Green Smock confirms it.

● ● ●

A few days later, when Blair and I get home from a walk around the block, there's a message on the answering machine from my cousin Kim. She is thirty-one years old and has five children, all under the age of six. The youngest is four months old and the only one she didn't give birth to naturally. Kim nursed them all. Kim home-schools them all. She told me several years ago that she and her husband believe it is their calling from God to be parents.

I know what has happened. My mother called Kim and asked her to call me, probably after I called my mother at her office yesterday afternoon and proceeded to cry, continuously, for fifty-three minutes about how I don't have time to do anything but hold the baby and we've eaten nothing but pizza for a week and the laundry is literally overflowing out of the hamper and I don't know what to do.

"Have you asked anyone for help?" my mother asked.

"No."

"Vicki, you have to ask for help."

"*Who* do I ask for help? Pompadour?"

I'd tried to line up some post-birth help. I talked Thad into hosting a neighborhood holiday party when I was six months pregnant, figuring the nine families on our block all needed to get better acquainted now that there was a baby on the way. In the two years we'd lived in the house, we'd only recently advanced to the level of neighborly intimacy that involved waving from cars as we pulled out of driveways. Maybe if they came into our home, if they saw what a warm shade of creamy brown we'd painted the family room, if we fed them beer and meatball sandwiches, they would see the pink "It's a Girl" balloon tied onto the front porch in a couple of months and bring over a casserole. I printed out invitations on special paper I bought at Kinko's, rolled them into tubes tied with shiny green bows, and placed them in everyone's mailbox, even inviting the lady in the white house on the corner whom we'd never actually seen in person. I bought pricey napkins at a gift store and dusted off the funny reindeer hors d'oeuvres plates my Aunt Bonnie gave us for Christmas last year. Thad bought exotic cheeses at the gourmet shop a few blocks away where the girl behind the counter flirts with him even when I'm there, and then made a party mix on his iPod that he plugged into the stereo in the family room. Nearly everyone came. And nearly everyone got drunk.

But hardly anyone seemed to notice when the baby arrived three months later. Whenever Blair and I took a walk, I'd often linger in front of the house with the stroller just to make sure that everyone on Melrose Avenue was clear that the "It's a Girl" balloon was genuine. The woman in the white Colonial across the street with two boys in college came over a few times to see Blair when we were sitting on the front porch. Another neighbor left a gift in our mailbox: a frilly dress with a matching hat. But they were the only ones. And we received not one casserole.

Toward the end of the call with my mom, I heard the call-waiting beep. It was my friend Candice checking in. Candice and I went to high school together, back when she still called herself Candie and we called ourselves "lust bunnies" as we obsessed over public school boys and went to the beach on Lake Erie as much as we could, primarily to be seen driving her brother's 1963 white convertible Dodge Dart. We hadn't really seen each other since, until about a year ago when she e-mailed me out of the blue to tell me she and her husband were moving just fifteen minutes from our house. That was fortunate for both of us since neither of us had any friends in New Jersey and since we both had dogs and husbands who played Xbox. Last week, after months and months and months of trying, Candice found out she was pregnant. When she called to tell me, I had to suck back in the words that were on the verge of spewing out of my mouth: *Are you sure you really want to do this?*

"That was Candie," I said to my mother when I clicked back to the other line.

"Did you ask her for help?"

"No."

An hour later the phone rang. It was Candice again. She and James were on their way over with tacos because she sensed all was not fine when I told her earlier, "All is fine. Blair's just crying all the time and I'm starving and there's no food in the house." They also brought baked ziti for us to eat over the weekend and two grocery bags filled with food I could eat with one hand—Hot Pockets, yogurt drinks, granola bars. I wanted to fall to my knees and massage their feet with oils. I sensed that Thad did too, when he walked in the door from work and found on the kitchen counter a buffet of seasoned meat and tortillas and shredded cheddar, next to a pan of brownies that Candice had just pulled out of the oven, in front of a wife who was laughing—actually laughing out loud—as she rolled up her burrito. James was holding Blair. Thad immediately walked over to rescue him.

"No, no, no," James said. "You eat." And Thad and I sat next to each other on the couch, eating a meal at the same time, which we hadn't been able to do for the past five weeks.

Now, the next day, buoyed both by last night's dinner and by the fact that Blair and I made it all the way around the block without a single cry from either of us, I feel prepared to call back my cousin Kim.

"How are youuuuu?" Kim asks in her always-chipper, singsong voice, ending her question, as she frequently does, with a reflexive giggle.

"I'm fine," I say, using my best, most awake, most I've-really-been-dying-to-talk-to-you voice. "Did my mom call you?"

"Yeaaaah, she did." Another giggle. I'm sure my mother thought Kim could advise me. My mother clearly forgot that Kim has five children, which means that, after the first one, she decided to have another. Clearly, Kim must have enjoyed this. Kim must have been good at this. And the last thing I need right now is someone counseling me on the joys and rewards of motherhood. "It's hard, Vicki," Kim says.

"Yeah, it's hard," I say, not sure if what she means by "hard" is what I mean by "hard." I tell her about the supplemental nurser, about the soy formula and how it hasn't stopped Blair from crying at all. I tell her how I keep looking in all my books to figure out what's going on and how all the books say different things so I don't know what to do. I don't tell her that I'm crying so much. And I certainly don't tell her why—that I've pretty much come to terms with the fact that I don't love my baby as much as I'm supposed to, and that I probably never will, and that's just the way it's going to be. In the background, I hear kids squealing and the creak of the chain on a swing. Kim is outside. With her children who, Kim explains, have all been sick with the flu this week. I feel like a jackass. Kim has five kids, including a four-month-old, all ailing with various degrees of flu, and she is not sitting Indian-style on the floor in her bedroom, naked, banging her head against the radiator. No, Kim is outside. I have one child who weighs less than 7 pounds and I count down every minute until Thad comes home so I can hand her off—*You deal with her*—and finally tend to the laundry basket that's been sitting in front of the TV since yesterday morning, folding onesie after onesie, so many I swear they breed and multiply in the wash.

"Vicki, can I say something?" Kim asks, gently, as if she's about to step into some no-man's-land of conversation that's likely to make us both uncomfortable. I suspect she's about to quote scripture. "Put the books away."

"What?"

"Just put the books away, Vicki. You have to follow your gut." I don't share that, earlier this week, my gut was telling me to leave Blair at Babies "R" Us and drive away.

"And you might want to stop using that supplemental nurser," she adds.

"Are you kidding? The doctor would kill me!" Now, I'm the one who's giggling because I seriously believe Dr. Weidner will kill me. Or, the next time we go in for a weight check, he'll press a big red button hidden under the exam table and an alarm will sound while a task force of men with "Child Services" pasted in black across their camouflage T-shirts will swoop in, grab Blair out of my arms, and leave in an un-marked van.

"Vicki, that nurser, it's just making you so upset. You can stop. You don't *have* to stop. That's not what I'm saying. But, if you want to, Vicki, you could try and stop and just see what happens."

"What do you mean, 'See what happens'? You mean, like, 'See if Blair starves to death'?"

Kim giggles. "Blair is not going to starve." Another giggle. "You might make more milk if you're not so stressed out about that thing."

"You think?"

"Maybe," Kim says. "I don't know. But, sometimes, you just have to do what you think is best. What *you*, Vicki . . . what *you* think is best."

I can vaguely remember a time not so long ago when I customarily did what I thought was best. When I trusted my instincts. However, my instincts seem to have slid out with the baby and are at the place, wherever it is, that they put all that extra stuff that slides out with the baby. This new, instinct-less me wants something the old me would never have tolerated: someone to tell her what to do. Kim says I need to do what I think is best. And what I think is best is *not* relying on what *I* think is best, but on what *Kim* thinks is best. None of Kim's children has starved. So if Kim thinks it's best to stop using the supplemental nurser, that's exactly what I'll do. I'll stop. Because Kim told me to.

"Thad, I really think it's best that I stop using the supplemental nurser," I declare when I get off the phone with Kim, assuming I'll have to convince him, because he'll be appalled, as if I've just suggested we remove Blair's tongue. He'll raise his right eyebrow. He'll say, "What do you mean, 'We'll see what happens'?" And I'll convince him that this is what my instincts are telling me to do, because I want him to believe that I still have instincts that still tell me what to do.

"Are you sure?" Thad asks.

"I'm sure."

"Okay. Whatever you think."

Okay? Did he just say "Okay"? Did he just say "Whatever you think," as if I just asked him if he thought we should stop having the *New York Times* delivered on Sundays? And, then, did he just walk away, down the hall to the bedroom, where he is now changing out of his work shirt?

"Are *you* sure?" I say as I stomp down the hall behind him, bouncing Blair in my arms, holding her off for a few seconds, even though I know she's ready to nurse.

"I'm sure if you're sure," Thad says, taking Blair so I can pee.

"Do you not have any opinion on this at all?" I ask crisply, staring up at him as I blot, cautiously, since I'm still afraid to *feel* anything down there. I still want an entire world of toilet paper between my fingers and my swollen girlfriend. Thad says nothing.

"Thad? Um . . . hellooo?" Again, Thad says nothing.

I know what's happening here—I'm taking Thad on because *I'm* not sure. I know Thad's relying on me to do what I think is best, because he wants someone to tell *him* what to do. And he's letting *me* tell him what to do, not understanding that I'm just pretending to know what to do. But I don't want him to know I'm pretending. So, instead, I get angry. At Thad. For leaving everything up to me and letting me do all the thinking and the deciding. For handing me all the responsibility for this child.

"For the record, she is your child, too," I say. I march out to the family room, strap on the My Brest Friend, and nurse without the nurser. Blair doesn't seem to notice. This should be a triumphant moment. It's not. I'm far too preoccupied with being mad at Thad, though I'm not entirely sure why. I'm just tired of being the only one feeling so bad all the time.

•　　　•　　　•

"You should go to that Baby and Me thing today," Thad warbles through a mouthful of oatmeal and brown sugar, which he is cramming in at warp speed, readying for his daily escape from my force field of hell.

"Is it today?" I ask. I know it's today. It's every Friday morning—9:30 to 11:30. I've known since the Prepared Childbirth Class we took at the hospital back in February, where I ate my continental breakfast and then finished off Thad's continental breakfast, not paying attention to the important things, like when to ask for the epidural. I was only concerned with what I'd been obsessing about since we found out I was pregnant—how to meet other new moms.

As soon as my belly officially popped, and Thad and I saw another pregnant couple, I'd nudge him in the ribs and whisper, "Go talk to them." At the movie theater. At Acme. At Home Depot. "Make friends with them. We need friends." Thad ignored me. But we did need friends. We needed married friends with babies, preferably first babies. Ideally, our new married-friends-with-babies would live in our neighborhood, and we would barbecue steaks together and go away together for long weekends in the Poconos in our popup campers and host New Year's parties where we'd stand around our piano and sing. So, when our instructor declared the first bathroom break of the morning, I stood up and announced to the other fifteen couples, "If anyone wants to exchange e-mails, we'd love to keep in touch." I waited through the rest of the class. I even loitered after, pretending to struggle with swaddling the baby doll we'd nicknamed Shirley while experimenting on her during the diapering demonstration. Not one person stopped by our table to give us a single e-mail address.

On our way home, while Thad scanned the roadside for a Taco Bell after I informed him that if I didn't eat a Nachos Bellgrande in the next 240 seconds I would likely pass out and die, I flipped through the handout from class. And there it was. On page six. A flyer for the weekly Baby and Me get-together at the community center next to the hospital, where "you will meet other new parents and support one another in your new roles."

I arrive to Baby and Me twenty-five minutes late because I had to try on five pairs of pants before I could admit to myself that the only non-sweatpants I owned that fit me were maternity jeans. The room is flanked by strollers. It smells like burned bagels and Wet Ones. There are about fifty women sitting in clusters on the floor, each with a baby wiggling on a blanket spread out in front of her—and not just any blanket, but homemade fleece ones with ties on the ends, and hand-embroidered ones, and expensive-looking pastel quilts ribbed with satin. I do not have a blanket with me. I do not even have a blanket in the minivan, where I wish I was right now.

I weave my stroller through the clusters, toward the line of empty chairs against the back wall. I kick down the brakes on the back wheels of the stroller, pull Blair out, sit on a chair, and nurse, which is so much less stressful now without the supplemental nurser and seems to be working just as well. In the past two weeks, Blair has gained a whole pound. Plus, nursing in this chair gets me off the hook, for the time being at least, of approaching one of the various sororities and asking if I can sit down and share one of their blankets, since I am a total sham who, if she were worth her weight in motherhood, would have an extra receiving blanket or a Kleenex or a breast pad somewhere in her diaper bag to protect her precious package of sugar and spice from the germy, drooly floor. I look up from my boob, grateful that Blair and I have succeeded in our first-ever public latching, to see that another woman has parked her stroller next to mine.

"Hi," I say.

"Hi," she says.

"Have you been here before?"

"Nope, this is my first time."

"Me too," I say. "I just got here. I was running really late because I couldn't find anything to wear that fit me."

"Oh, my God! Me too!" she says. I decide that this woman is my new best friend. I *knew* this would happen. I *knew* that, if I just met some other new moms who were dealing with the very same things I was dealing with, I'd discover that everything I'd been going through was normal, that everyone was feeling exactly the same way I was.

My new best friend lifts her son out of his stroller. He is a vision in light blue: light-blue pants, a light-blue sweatshirt with an appliqué of a baseball and bat on the left pocket, light-blue socks, white sneakers with light-blue stripes, and a light-blue baseball cap with a brown puppy on it next to the words "Bark! Bark!" Blair is wearing what she always wears—a long-sleeved white onesie that hangs 2 inches past her fingertips, pink-striped reversible infant pants, and a pair of yellow socks that look like they would probably fit Thad. She is, as usual, swaddled in a receiving blanket, because she is significantly less miserable when swaddled, even more so now since she probably knows it's preventing Little Boy Blue and his mom from seeing how homeless her outfit looks. Little Boy Blue is very chubby. He is so big that he looks like he's around a year old.

"How old is he?" I ask.

"Three weeks," she says.

"Three weeks? You're kidding."

"Three weeks," she says again. I wait. Maybe I'm wrong, but the etiquette seems rather obvious—I ask you how old your kid is; you ask me how old my kid is. I wait a minute more.

"My daughter is six weeks," I say. "She's a peanut."

"Wow," the mom says, as she hefts her 72-pound, three-week-old son onto the crocheted light blue blanket she's spread out on the floor. "Jackson weighed 9 pounds, 7 ounces when he was born, and he pretty much hasn't stopped eating since. He just eats and eats and eats. His father says he knew my num-nums would keep his big boy happy, and I knew it too, ever since he latched on the first try at the hospital, I mean the nurses couldn't believe what a well-tempered baby he was and I figured Jackson could just tell that I loved him so darn. . . . "

I think it was around "eats and eats and eats" that I noticed that this woman has eye shadow on, which matches her beige velour sweat suit. When she flipped her long black hair at "num-nums," I could smell her shampoo.

". . . so the doctor was just as surprised as I was that he regained his birth weight before we even left the hospital and at his well-baby visit yesterday he was already in the ninety-fifth percentile. The ninety-fifth percentile! And do you know what his father said when we got home? He said, 'Why isn't he at the one-hundredth percentile?' Isn't that so funny? Daddy just wants you to be perfect in every way, my little stinky-winky Jackson Wackson. . . . "

I know that Blair will be sucking for forty-five or so more minutes but, in my head, I plan my escape. I will wave at a random mother across the room and say something like, "I can't believe she's here! I'll be right back," and then carry over Blair, still attached, sit down and explain that I had to break free from this woman's gravitational pull of Madonna-and-childness. Or I'll stand up abruptly, claiming that Blair has just spit up her intestines, and rush to the bathroom, where I'll wait it out until 11:30 in a stall. Or I'll lure some other nearby mother into our conversation.

"I'm sorry," I say to the blonde woman sitting a few feet away from us in a circle of other blonde women with blonde babies. "I was eavesdropping and I thought I heard you say something about movies for mommies . . . " Just as the blonde woman opens her mouth to explain, Madonna speaks up in a voice so loud that people living in the Ukraine can probably hear her.

"Oh, yes, the movies at the Loews in Cherry Hill. Jackson and I went last Tuesday. They turn down the volume and turn up the lights and set up a changing table. It's still as dirty as it usually is. I mean, those floors are so sticky I was afraid that Jackson was going to drop his paci and then what . . . "

I look at the blonde mommy, expecting to catch her eye and then subtly roll my own to say, "Can you *believe* this woman?" But the blonde mommy is listening, very rapt, as if Madonna is, in fact, engaging. And normal. And I realize that I was absolutely wrong. These mothers are not feeling what I'm feeling. I am not like them. I am not like any mother. I really *am* completely alone in this.

"Holy hell," I say, standing up. "My daughter just spit up all over herself." I dump Blair into her stroller, hoping no one notices that she's as clean as the very well-flossed spaces between Madonna's teeth, then throw everything that belongs to us into the stroller, which I career out of the room faster than I can say "Jackson Wackson."

•   •   •

The following Tuesday, I drive around the parking lot at the Loews movie theater, wondering why there are no other cars. Maybe Madonna lied to me. And to think I woke up this morning actually hoping she and Little Boy Blue would be here so I'd have someone to sit with. Just then, I see a woman backing out of the door, thrashing about as she fights to glide her stroller out at the same time. I park. I push my stroller up the wheelchair ramp and right over to the woman who is rocking her stroller back and forth, checking the time on her cell phone.

"I was just about to leave. I didn't think anyone was here," I say.

"That's why I came out," she says, laughing. "I saw you driving around and I thought you were thinking exactly what I was . . . that there was no one here." I'm amazed at how precisely the liner around her lips matches her spiky auburn hair. Her nails are fake and painted a very 1986 pink frost. She has a sword tattooed around her ankle.

"When was your daughter born?" I ask.

"March 9th. How about yours?"

"March 16th! How crazy is *that?*" I say the word "that" far too loud.

"I have a friend coming whose daughter was born March 20th."

"That is just *nuts!*" Again, too loud. "Can I sit with you guys?"

"Sure," she says. Her name is Nancy. She's older than I am, closer to forty. Her daughter's name is Bella, short for Isabella Rose, named after a mountain in Italy and the enchanted rose in *Beauty and the Beast.* I notice that Nancy is talking a little loudly herself and I wonder if it's a sign that she's excited to meet me in the same way that I'm excited to meet her, even though I'm pretending I'm not that excited to meet her—another new mom who just picked up the pacifier that her daughter jettisoned onto the ground, licked off the dirt, and put it back in Bella's mouth. I don't want Nancy to think I'm weird and desperate and likely to call her at two in the morning to reflect on the consistency of Blair's most recent poop. "And, you know," Nancy says, "after the movie, we were thinking about walking over to T.G.I. Friday's to have lunch, if you want to come."

I look across the parking lot to T.G.I. Friday's. I've never taken Blair to a restaurant before. A scene flashes in my head. I'm zigzagging around tables, shushing Blair, bouncing Blair, while men in business suits glare up from their Chicken Finger BLTs and announce, just loud enough to be sure I can hear them: *Can't that woman control that child?*

I want to say *no.* I start to say it, but I stop myself. I can't say no. I have to do this. This is my chance to get new-mom friends. I need to go for it, since every other expectation I had about motherhood has disappeared into the reeking depths of the Diaper Genie. And if I'm not going to have the experience of sitting in the park next to the blooming forsythias, staring down at this gorgeous child free of smells and sin and baby acne, overcome by a love that is so intense it literally makes my heart burn, then I will at least have lunch at T.G.I. Friday's with other new moms. And here they are, right here, our kids born during the same eleven-day stretch, me with a family pack of Twizzlers I bought at Target over the weekend. I have to go to T.G.I. Friday's.

"That sounds cool," I say, and we stroll inside to buy tickets. The other mom—Jenn—and her daughter—Cailyn—meet us in line. Jenn is wearing black sweatpants and her hair is twisted in a ponytail. She looks like I feel, tired but relieved that she's not sitting on her couch for the fifty-fifth day in a row. Or maybe she's just excited to see Ashton Kutcher in *A Lot Like Love.* I'm excited to see Ashton Kutcher. Ashton Kutcher is on my list of men I'm allowed to cheat on Thad with if presented with the opportunity. If the tables were turned and it were Ashton looking out of the screen into the movie theater dotted with moms and babies, smelling like diaper, watching me as I shift in my seat to find a position to nurse Blair that doesn't feel like she might slip, headfirst, through the space between the seat and the armrest, I doubt he would present me with the opportunity.

Strangely, though, I hardly even notice Ashton. Or the movie. Because, for the past forty-five minutes, Blair nursed. Calmly. Without crying. And Blair has fallen asleep in my arms.

Blair is asleep.

In my arms.

Cailyn has also fallen asleep. Nancy is wiping spit-up off her shoulder. Other kids are crying. Blair—my Blair—is asleep. I can't stop looking at her, and feeling proud as I look at her, at those long eyelashes fanned out under her lids, at the slight blush in her cheeks, at the smoothness of her skin, which I rarely see since her face is so often winced in some phase of distress. I wish I had the camera. I wish I could take a photo of her right now, download it when I get home, and e-mail it this afternoon for today's edition of *The Daily Blair*. I'd been sending photos of Blair to Thad and his parents and my parents not-quite-so-daily ever since I stopped the supplemental nurser, figuring at the time that I could neutralize a Bad Mommy Act by performing a Good Mommy Act. Even though Blair still didn't do much except impersonate a bag of flour, and even though she had no idea I was anything more important to her than a milk truck, I felt it was my duty to take one photo of her a day—Blair in her swing "awake and not crying," Blair being held by our friend Dave, "entertaining gentlemen callers." A photo of her right now would be endearing. Calm. Sleeping. Serene. Just like babies are supposed to be.

But Blair wakes up. She wakes up as we're crossing the parking lot to T.G.I. Friday's. She wakes up mad, flailing, while I pop wheelies with the stroller hoping to placate her. She barks all the way through the door, all the way to the table in the back corner. I reach in my diaper bag and pull out the sling I got in the mail a few days ago, the one my friend Jenny said I *"must* have." It's a solid piece of black fabric that I fold in half, making a round tube that I slip over one shoulder, leaving a crevice in front of my chest. I've only successfully stuffed Blair into this thing once, at home last night, in front of a mirror, so I'm well aware that shoving her in the gap and then jiggling the fabric until her whole body disappears into it looks vaguely like child abuse. But I do it. And I stand. And I bounce. And she stays quiet, giving me a little break, letting me eat my Santa Fe Chicken Salad and savor my Diet Coke, which I've been fantasizing about drinking for the past eleven months, ever since I found out I was pregnant and went cold turkey on caffeine.

"Did anyone else tell their husband they weren't allowed to have sex yet?" Nancy asks.

"What do you mean?" Jenn says.

"I had my six-week follow-up at the OB and the doctor gave me the green light for sex, but when I got home I told Dave, 'Guess what? The doctor says we have to wait another couple weeks.' I am *so* not in the mood." My six-week appointment is in two days. I'm so relieved I discovered this ploy in time.

"Oh my God! I did the same thing," Shane says. Shane is a co-worker of Nancy's. She was also at the movie. Her daughter, Jillian, was born March 1. Just then, Jillian starts to cry.

Blair must hear Jillian crying, because she starts to cry, too. I look around the restaurant. It's full of businessmen. I start to panic. I stand up and bounce, but it does no good. I sit down, unleash my boob. Blair latches on. But she keeps whimpering. Jillian is crying louder than Blair, and Shane's face is turning red. I notice, then, how pretty Shane is, like a model, blonde hair held back off her forehead with a scarf, ice-blue eyes. And she is skinny, her tummy already flat, her butt already contracting back to normal dimensions, which are, for Shane, those of a thirteen-year-old. Shane has ordered a broiled chicken breast with steamed broccoli on the side, which she isn't eating because her face is red and her daughter's face is red and everyone is acting like they haven't noticed. I wonder if she's feeling what I'm feeling. I wonder if she's looking at these other babies, asleep in their strollers, none of them making a single sound this entire day so far, and feeling jealous. And a little ripped off. *Why do* they *get such sweet babies? Why do* they *get to enjoy this time?*

Nancy mentions that Bella used to cry like that, until the doctor realized she had acid reflux and put her on Zantac. Shane isn't listening as she pulls out a bottle, fills it with water, dumps in four ounces of powdered Similac, stirs it up, and puts it in Jillian's mouth. Jillian stops crying. Instantly. Jillian was hungry. Blair, still whining after fifteen full minutes of nursing, glances over at Jillian, then looks back at me as if to say, "Remember the good old days with the supplemental nurser when I wasn't starving to death on your crappy boobs?"

And here, in T.G.I. Friday's, I enter a new stage in the unrelenting crisis of confidence I've been flailing in for the past seven weeks. *Why am I breastfeeding this child?* Even though she gained a little weight this week? Even though practically everyone I know who had a baby in the past two years breastfed? Even though every parenting magazine that came free to my house during my pregnancy preached about how women are "made" to breastfeed? Even though the lactation consultant at the hospital proclaimed, "It's your *job* to feed this baby." Haven't there been plenty of other signs that I should bag it? The jaundice. The weight loss. The supplementing. The crying. In an odd moment of self-defense, the voice in my head shouts out: *You're doing this for her! Breastfeeding boosts her immune system. It protects her from allergies and obesity and all kinds of awful diseases. It might even make her smarter. This is for Blair. You're doing all this for Blair.*

But as much as I need to believe I'm doing this one, selfless, good-mom thing for my daughter, I know that's not true. I know the real reason, the one that, once I slide into the driver's seat of the minivan, lets loose a wave of tears down my cheeks. I barely get my sunglasses on in time to hide my eyes while I wave to Nancy as she pulls away. By the time I get to the traffic light at the edge of the parking lot, my shoulders have collapsed in on my chest. I can barely see.

Why am I breastfeeding this child?

For *me.*

Because, when I'm breastfeeding this child, I at least feel connected to her. If I stop, then what? What will we have? What will exist between this mother and this child?

Nothing?

Is that possible?

never let them see you mother

"You probably know much more than you think you do about being a parent."

—*Caring for Your Baby and Young Child:
Birth to Age 5*

I park the minivan in the lot under my office building in Philadelphia, jostle Blair's car seat into the stroller, and steer down 18th Street to Rittenhouse Square park, where I'm meeting my friend Rebecca. Rebecca just had a baby too, Carolyn, who is two months older than Blair and, reportedly, a disgustingly pleasant child.

I feel like I'm not supposed to be here—not the "me" who has a two-month-old baby, whose enormous purple and black stroller is taking up way too much space on the city sidewalk crammed with people in suits, talking on cell phones, maneuvering to pass me as fast as they can. The me that was last here, walking down this street from the building on the corner, from the office on the thirty-sixth floor, was not a mom. That me was third-in-command at a magazine. That me managed people, made decisions, was generally liked by the people she spent her days with. And I'm counting on the fact that she's still up there, waiting, and six weeks from now, I'll ride the train into work, take the elevator up, and step back into her skin. I'll be who I was before.

"Oh my God . . . hey!" I'm suddenly stroller-to-face with one of the very perky, very blonde, very stylish girls who works as an advertising assistant at the magazine. I can't remember her name, but I suspect that she's closer to Blair's age than to mine. She peeks into the stroller, and says, again, "Oh. My. God!"

"It's crazy, isn't it?" I say.

"Are you having, like, so much fun?" she asks, literally hopping up and down.

"No," I say. Her eyebrows crumple together, as if I just told her that I'm really a man. I grin. I'm proud of myself. I said it out loud. Finally. *No, I am not having so much fun. No, this totally sucks. No, I hate it.*

"See ya," I say, waving as I push along.

Rebecca and I find an empty bench in the park, next to the fountain. Surprisingly, Blair is sleeping. Rebecca's daughter is screaming. I feel more satisfied by this than I should. No matter which angle Rebecca tries, Carolyn won't latch onto her breast, jolting her head away as if the milk tastes sour. When I glance up at Rebecca's face, I see an expression I recognize completely. It's the same desperate look I've seen staring back at me in the mirror for the past two months.

"Sometimes . . ." Rebecca pauses, her voice raspy as if what she's about to say physically hurts her throat. She looks over her shoulder, then down at her sandwich. "Sometimes . . . I just . . . want . . . to tell her . . . to . . . shut up." Rebecca lowers her head, as if waiting for me to pull the tube of Desitin out of my diaper bag and flog her with it. Instead, I stand up. I open my mouth wide like I'm about to sing a very high note. I stick out my arms, ready to hug her.

"Sometimes I *do!* Sometimes I *do* tell her to shut up!" I yell.

"Sometimes I tell her to shut up, *too!*" Rebecca yells.

I freeze. I wait for her to backpedal, to recant, to say "Just kidding" or "I feel so bad about it" or "Good thing I love her so much." But she doesn't. She doesn't say anything. She's staring, too, probably waiting for me to say something. Or waiting for the gang of nannies sitting across the park by the bronze goat statue to parade over and ram their strollers into ours.

"I thought it was just me," I say.

"Me too," Rebecca says. She laughs, hesitantly. "I never expected this all to be so hard."

"Me neither," I say, overcome with an elusive emotion. It's not quite redemption. It's more like vindication, like the obscene amount of frustration I've felt over this teeny-tiny child hasn't been my fault. I'm not a bad person after all.

Carolyn is crying harder now. Rebecca sets her jaw. I wonder if she's trying to keep herself from crying, since she looks like she's about to cry. I feel a ball in my throat, too, like *I* might very well start to cry. I'm relieved when Rebecca announces she should probably go home, so she can sit in her rocker and prop up Carolyn on pillows and "get this feeding done."

She walks away, then turns back.

"Good thing I'm so crazy in love with this little girl," she says, so sincerely, that I swear the world around us stops short. Nothing moves. And I'm back in that place where I was this morning and the day before—in that dark, lonely hole.

•   •   •

"It's about time," my friend Melissa says when Thad and I push the stroller though the doors to the ballroom at the Hilton in Columbia, Maryland. We are an hour and a half late to her wedding reception. We are so late that the thought of not going in at all crossed my mind in the minivan moments ago, as I slipped into the hot pink tank top I bought to wear primarily because it was so low-cut I assumed people would be too dazzled by my unprecedented cleavage to notice that the rest of my body—including my knees—still appears to be five months pregnant.

"Sorry," I say, hugging her. "It took longer than we thought it would."

I tried to get out of this. I tried to convince myself Melissa wouldn't care—it was basically just a big party since the couple eloped last fall in St. John. I e-mailed Melissa last week to explain that we probably wouldn't make it, even though I was practically responsible for this marriage—my college friend Melissa met my high school friend John at the drunken party after our wedding two years ago. Melissa wrote back immediately: "But we decided to have it that day *because* you said you could be there that day! You *said!*" The reason we said we could be there that day was because I was still pregnant when we said it, back when we imagined it would be a fun adventure to take a day trip as a new family, back when the baby was still a theoretical baby. Theoretical babies slept for the entire 121-mile drive down I–95. Theoretical babies didn't wake up to nurse twenty-two minutes into the trip. Theoretical babies didn't scream for the rest of the drive while theoretical mommies "shushed" in their ears and shook the car seat, violently, for two hours straight, hoping the movement would make the theoretical baby think she was being bounced around her theoretical yellow house in New Jersey.

I try to explain this to Melissa, but she isn't listening. Melissa is lifting Blair out of the stroller, drawing Blair in tight against her shoulder. I'm glad that Melissa's wearing a black cotton sundress and not an intricate wedding gown that wouldn't stand up very well to curdled breast-milk puke.

"I can't believe you have a baby," Melissa says to me as she instinctively sways back and forth, her arms wrapped around Blair's tiny shoulders and thighs. Blair looks precious in the white-flowered Ralph Lauren dress with the cap sleeves and matching panties, which she finally weighs enough to kind of fit into. Blair isn't crying. But I swear she's about to. I swear I see the blue vein on her forehead starting to swell.

"*You* can't believe I have a baby?" I say. I know what Melissa means. She can't believe this person she took surfing lessons with in Hawaii has a baby. She can't believe this person who up and quit her first real magazine job to move to Colorado "just because I feel like it" has a baby. She can't believe this person she watched hitch a ride during a Harley Davidson parade with a man wearing a Viking hat with foot-long horns sticking out of it has a baby. What I mean, though, is that I can't believe that I *have* a baby, that I literally have a baby in my possession, that someone hasn't come and taken her away from me by now.

And yet, for the hour and a half we spend at this reception, I don't have a baby. Thad doesn't have a baby either. Melissa has the baby. My friend Meghan from high school who is six months pregnant has the baby. Amy from college has the baby and has taken the baby for a walk somewhere. I know should feel like I've been handed a get-out-of-jail-free card. I don't. My breath keeps catching, pulsing, in short, quick gulps of air, as my eyes dart around the room, looking for Amy, afraid that Blair's freaking out and Amy doesn't know what to do, because she wants to give the baby back to me but feels bad about it since I haven't yet taken a single bite of my stuffed chicken. Ten minutes later, I spot Amy. Amy doesn't have the baby. Melissa's mom has the baby. And the baby is still not crying.

"What kind of spell did you people put on my child?" I ask her as I shovel the last bite of a piece of carrot cake into my mouth.

"You smell of milk," Melissa's mother says.

"What?" I turn away fast, looking down at my pink chiffon shirt, certain I'm going to find big, dark, wet circles expanding over my boobs.

"You smell of milk. I don't. When she smells milk, she gets hungry and starts to cry."

"Is that so," I say. "I thought she was just saving up energy for the ride." Because this isn't the end of our trip. A certain theoretical mommy had this great idea back when she was still pregnant—instead of driving home from this party, we will drive to Erie and stay with the theoretical grandparents for a week or so, while the theoretical daddy flies back home to work, then flies back and chauffeurs his theoretical family home. According to MapQuest, the drive will take eight hours and two minutes plus two more hours to account for two nursings. At least.

"Vic, we need to get on the road," Thad whispers in my ear, as we stand outside the hotel on a patio next to the ballroom, while someone takes the first photo of our little family since we were sitting together on the bed at the hospital eight weeks ago. It's just after 5:00 PM when I announce that we must leave, that we're driving to my parents' house in Erie. I hear a woman behind me gasp. Melissa's mother theatrically falls back into a chair, then stands up, insisting we stay at her house for the night.

"Oh, no," I say. "That's very kind, but, no."

"That's such a long drive," she says.

"I know. Boy . . . do I know."

"I'm not sure the baby can handle it."

Stooooooooooop! I scream in my head, then spin around to make sure that the scream was, in fact, in my head, that I didn't just yell "Stop!" at the bride's mom.

Thad and I hug and handshake and do the cheek-kiss thing. I fantasize about the black sweat suit I tucked into the storage compartment under the stroller, about the flip flops, about changing into it all in the bathroom down the hall, about falling asleep in the backseat, under the red fleece blanket we keep in the van for emergencies. I need to sleep. I can feel it in my eyes, as if there's sandpaper taped to the inside of my eyelids, scraping at each blink, reminding me that I haven't slept more than an hour at a stretch in more than two months. It's been my choice—to let Thad sleep as much as he can so he's able to function at work. But now the back of my neck hurts, too. And my temples. And my spine. It aches there, in all the important parts, like my body is threatening to fold in on itself.

Before we pull out of the parking garage, I nurse Blair in the backseat. As soon as I unhook the strap on the white nursing tank, Blair curls her body around my chest. She shimmies in, like she can't get close enough to me, like she's trying to soak into my skin. She's never done this before.

"Thad, I think she's nuzzling," I yell up to the front, where Thad's adjusting his seat. "She almost looks like she might like me."

"Vicki, she likes you." Of course he says this. He isn't around all day long. He doesn't witness her general reaction to my existence, which is just about the same level of affection that I express to a can of French-cut green beans.

Twenty-six minutes later, all this mommy-baby-bonding flushes out though the air vents and flattens like roadkill on Route 70. Blair has let loose. But this doesn't sound like our average, everyday cry. Or maybe it is. Maybe it just sounds more threatening in the cramped confines of the van, during the first twenty-six minutes of a ten-plus-hour trip. I read last week in *Touchpoints: The Essential Reference Guide for the Early Years* that I was supposed to be able to tell the difference between Blair's cries by the time she was three weeks old—between the morning cry and the evening cry, the hungry cry and the peed-though-my-diaper cry, the hold-me cry and the my-stomach-feels-like-it-might-have-fallen-out cry. I've tried. I've even put my ear right up to her quaking face when she's in that high-pitched, wild-beast-caught-in-a-trap zone, the one that makes me want to run to her and away from her at the exact same speed, but I still can't tell. Every cry sounds the same to me. Every one is loud. Every one is exasperating. Every one makes me want to plug my ears.

"You never cried like that," my mother told me when I called Sunday night to ask what I should do.

"Thad never cried like that," my mother-in-law told me last night, when she called as we were packing and heard Blair screeching in the background while Thad walked her around the house, passing me at every lap with a pleading expression on his face that begged me to tell him what to do. "His brother didn't cry like that either," she added. Neither did any baby I'd ever come across, nor any baby I'd ever heard about from my friends or my cousins or anyone, nor any baby I'd ever seen on the Learning Channel. Babies are not supposed to cry this much. Not *this* much. This is not the way it's supposed to be.

But there is something about this cry—this cry that's practically sucking up all the air in the van—that sounds particularly strange, particularly fierce. As if she's hurting. And I have a thought I've not yet considered in the past two months—*What if there is something wrong with her?*

On the day my water broke, I was writing an article for *Philadelphia* magazine about the parents of a girl named Alex who had cancer and, who, all by herself, started a lemonade-stand charity that grew and grew until she'd raised millions of dollars for pediatric cancer research. She died when she was six, but her parents kept the lemonade stands going, which was why I was writing about them, why I'd been interviewing them at their home on a Wednesday evening when I was eight months pregnant. I asked Alex's mom, Liz, when she realized that something was wrong with Alex, needing the information for the story but also wanting to know for myself.

Was there something I should look for? How would I know?

"She was a real cranky baby," Liz said. "She never slept. . . . She seemed uncomfortable. I kept saying to the doctors, 'It seems like something is bothering her, something is hurting her.'"

This conversation comes flooding back to me now, as Blair is crying like something is hurting her. I shake the car seat harder, praying she's not hurting, praying she'll stop, praying I will shake this thought out of my head because I can't bear to let it rest there even for a second more. The thought alone makes my chest contract in on itself, makes me feel this heavy, thick mass spread out in my torso and start to choke my throat. I can't look at Blair. I can't allow this thought, this mass, this story to connect to her, to this child whom I've barely told "I love you" but whose very life, I discover here in the car, here at this moment, is very clearly, very inexplicably more important to me than my own.

But the thought of the creeping, evil illness I decide she's harboring in one of her tiny organs disappears as soon as we pass through Frederick. I hear the rain before I see it, hammering down on the metal roof of the van in sporadic, thick drops as if parts of the sky have started to fall. The sound quickly increases to machine-gun fire, pounding so loud I can't hear anything else—not the engine, not the windshield wipers, not Thad, not the baby. Minutes pass. My ears adjust. I still can't hear the baby. I also can't see the baby. The downpour has snapped the day into twilight. The only lights I see are headlights, refracting all across the sudden sea of highway, beating the undercarriage of the van so we're getting it now from all sides. Thad is driving too fast. He's passing everyone. I'm about to shout up to remind him that there is precious cargo in this car and that my mother will kill him with her bare hands if anything happens to one single cell of any of it, when a beam from an exit ramp light shines into the backseat, illuminating Blair's face for barely a second.

Blair is sleeping.

I grab onto the back of Thad's seat and pull myself forward in super slow motion so as not to risk even the slightest movement waking this child.

"She's sleeping," I whisper.

"What?" Thad says, full voice.

"Shhhhh." I cut him off. "She's sleeping."

"She's sleeping?"

She keeps sleeping, through the rain, through Thad turning up the air conditioning all the way to defog the windows, through me shutting the vents above her, covering her with the purple and pink fleece blanket my grandmother's hairdresser made for her, through me digging around the floor for the red fleece blanket for myself, through the rain stopping as abruptly as it began.

"Can you turn down the air?" I whisper to Thad. "It's freezing."

He does. And, just as I recline my seat, anticipating the nap I'd been dreaming of since March 16 at 2:06 in the afternoon, Blair starts to cry again. And, though I grit my teeth real, real hard, I start to cry too.

All of a sudden, the air flips back on.

"It's *cold*," I say, leaning forward, talking louder than I should to make sure he can hear me over the air conditioning hushing out of the vents, not paying attention to what I can't hear over the hushing—Blair.

She's fallen back to sleep. Just like that.

"It's the noise," Thad explains, catching my eye in the rearview mirror. "She likes the noise."

I lean back, amazed at how quickly Thad figured this out, knowing that this discovery might just change my life.

She likes the noise.

She likes something.

•   •   •

Guests start arriving at my parents' house just before two on Sunday, May 21, for Blair's Coming Out Party, a week after we arrived in Erie. My mother planned it at the last minute, inviting her friends and neighbors, all the people she's been celebrating with for years and years over the birth of grandchild after grandchild while she teased her unmarried daughter, "You know, you don't *need* to get married to have a baby"—except that she kind of meant it. Blair isn't in much of a party mood, despite the fact that she's wearing her party outfit, a denim jumper with a red plaid Peter Pan collar. I'm wearing a red nursing tank that barely covers the elastic band on my maternity jeans. I'm also hiding. I'm on the couch downstairs in the family room, giving Blair a quick snack, hoping it might make her slightly more social. It doesn't. She wails and, instantly, the wail acts as a siren, summoning all women to the presence of the wailing baby, a procession marching single-file down the steps as if on a rescue mission.

"Here she is," I say, introducing my child, already bouncing as I stand up, which softens Blair's bellow a few decibels. "She's in a mood," I explain, though I'm the one who is in the mood. I'm too exhausted to explain one more time to one more person that yes, it does seem like Blair cries a lot, and no, the doctor hasn't diagnosed her with colic or allergies or bird flu, and yes, we've tried gas drops, and yes, we've tried Gripe Water, and yes, we've tried Zantac, and no, we haven't given up breastfeeding and switched to formula.

Earlier in the week, after we first arrived and Thad flew back home, I felt like an entirely different person, like I'd died and gone to Gwyneth Paltrow's house where there were so many nannies running around I could eat a piece of peanut-butter toast in the morning while I scribbled thank-you notes without a baby attached to me. My mother took the week off from work. My dad's mom drove over once a day, usually with a Tupperware container full of pigs-in-a-blanket or meatloaf or cut-up carrots floating in water. My father took over when he came home from work, Blair's tiny body reclining in his big Poppy arms, looking forward, a hold Thad named "the front of the tour bus." And my other grandmother, known to her eight great-grandchildren as Gigi, was there, staying with us full-time since my mom picked her up a few days ago in Pittsburgh, where she lives.

In the mornings, I walked and bounced Blair in preparation for her late-morning nap, nursing her at the same time, because now, in Erie, she would only nurse without crying if I simultaneously walked around while bouncing her up and down. So I walked and bounced in a track around the main floor of my parents' house, from the kitchen to the living room to the dining room where, on the table, my mother set up Blair's diaper-changing station on a thick, folded bath towel, next to a stack of Pampers and a plastic container of wipes, little stuffed toys and crystals hanging from the chandelier on strings of gold Christmas yarn so they dangled just above Blair's head. When Blair was lying there, getting wiped down, she'd throw her arms up toward the purple-and-orange striped bee. She gurgled like she not only knew what the bee was, but she was excited to see the bee. Her lips curled in a funny way. My mother said she was smiling, which, if I could believe her, would be the first time I'd ever seen my baby intentionally smile.

Every day, Gigi took over for a nap shift, sitting on the rocking chair in the family room downstairs, the blinds drawn, the TV tuned to her soap, holding Blair. She'd hold her for hours, rocking back and forth, readjusting Blair's position—from her chest, to her shoulder, to across her arms, Blair on her stomach with her bald head tucked under Gigi's armpit—patient in the way an eighty-eight-year-old woman can be patient with a fussy infant because she truly has nothing else to do. And every day, I'd take a few photos of them, though I didn't really need to. Gigi was doing just fine, even though the doctor had given her one year to live six years ago, and her lung cancer hardly appeared to be growing. Even though every time one of her granddaughters announced she was pregnant, Gigi told everyone, "Well I guess I have to hold on until the baby is born," and my youngest cousin Becky's baby wasn't due until November. Most of the photos were exactly the same as the photos I'd shot the day before, Blair's face knotted up, Gigi not looking at the camera. I pretended there was something different, though, acting as if Blair was making an unusual face or that they were in a slightly cuter position than on Monday, just so it wasn't so obvious—that I was taking this photo in case it might be the last one of my grandmother and my child together. Despite the fact that I knew that Gigi knew exactly why I was taking it.

Gigi appears to be the only woman in the house who hasn't come down to the family room to see what all the wailing is about, who isn't swarming around us. During the past week, Gigi has gotten used to this. She knows how this goes.

"Oh, let me take her," Mrs. Blake says, reaching out.

"She's really tough," I murmur, feeling my cheeks get prickly, not sure if I'm embarrassed because I have this baby that I can't let another person hold without first issuing a warning or because I'm incapable of making this baby pleasant enough to be held.

"I've been through *this* before," Mrs. Blake says. And I realize I've been gauging this party all wrong. I shouldn't be irritated. I should be rejoicing. I should be jumping up and down in the midst of all these mothers and grandmothers with all their motherly and grandmotherly experience. They can help me. They'll know what to do. Mrs. Blake has two kids and six grandchildren. And, if not her, then Mrs. Neithamer should have a suggestion, with three kids of her own and seven grandchildren. Or our neighbor, Mrs. Newcomb, with four kids, two grandchildren, several dogs, and one bird. I watch carefully as Mrs. Blake flips Blair—who is swaddled so tightly in her purple-and-green-striped receiving blanket that no one can see her sweet party outfit anyway—onto her stomach on Mrs. Blake's arm.

"This is called the colic hold," Mrs. Blake says.

"Yeah. . . . " I answer, expectantly, waiting for another sentence, another phrase of advice that takes the colic hold to a whole new level for me. Because of course I know the colic hold. Of course I've tried the colic hold, hourly, for almost two and a half months. Mrs. Blake doesn't say another word. She just stands there, colic-holding. And Blair cries. And cries. And cries. And no one says anything, staring at Mrs. Blake, whose forehead is wrinkling. She looks hugely confused, like she's a bit embarrassed herself, disappointed in herself, afraid she can't actually do this thing she so confidently claimed she could do. I'm far too familiar with that feeling to allow her or anyone else to stand here, struggling with my child, wondering, *Why can't I do this?*

"Ohhhhh," I hum, lifting Blair out of her arms, trying not to sound as let down as I feel that even a room filled with experience can't help me. "I have a feeling that what this little girl wants right now is something you can't give her." I plop back down on the couch and toss a blanket over my shoulder, as if it's time to nurse. The room clears instantly. Blair stops crying

instantly. I look down at her face to see if she's choking. Why else would she stop crying like that? But
she's not choking. She tilts her head onto my chest,
her left hand poking up out of the swaddle, spreading
out her fingers on my collar bone, like an almost-hug.
I don't move. I don't want to move ever again. I want
my mother to sneak down and take a picture of us so
we can put it in Blair's baby album, this photo that
everyone else has, the one of the peaceful mommy
with the peaceful baby falling asleep on her bosom.
We need to remember this moment. I need to remember it.

I hear my mother's voice upstairs, regaling someone
about the problem we've all been laboring with since my
very first ultrasound—what will this baby call her? She
always thought she'd be "Grammy." She'd called her
grandmother "Grammy." Except that Thad's niece,
who is thirteen years old, already calls Thad's mother
"Grammy," leaving my mother without a name of her
own. Since her name is Judy, I suggested "Juju." She
thought it sounded racist. She suggested "Grandy."
I thought it sounded fat. "Grandma" was too ordinary.
"Nana" seemed more like a name for a private part. And
just as my mother was threatening to refer to herself,
simply, as "The Grandmother Who Drinks Wine," we
had an idea.

"Grudy!" My mother proclaims, as I clog up the
steps to join the conversation.

"Grudy?" My Aunt Elaine asks, as if my mother just declared she'd be calling herself Crapface.

"Like 'grandma' and 'Judy' in one," I explain to the room, unable to discern to whom, exactly, my mother is speaking, since the revelation of this special title, punctuated by my mother's large and enthusiastic arm gestures, has caused all heads to turn. I take advantage of the attention.

"Heeeeeere's Blaaaaair," I say, smiling big and exaggerated as I do every time Blair and I venture into public, as if I'm on stage, playing "mother," playing "happy," playing "so wide awake that I'd never, ever be able to lie down right here on this floor, right here on your shoes, and pass out." This time, though, I'm so exaggerated that I startle Blair, her eyelids fluttering as she cocks open her mouth to let go. I pull the pacifier out of my pocket. I still carry it. I've watched the babies of my mommy friends spend all 140 minutes of *Star Wars Episode 3* sucking away. I've seen their happy faces. Pacifiers make those kids happy. I want my kid to be happy. If she's happy, I'll be happy. If she's happy, I'll have no excuse not to be happy.

"Oh my God," I sigh to myself, as this child in my arms, for the first time ever, clamps onto the pacifier like it's coated in cocaine. *We did it*, I think. *We finally did it*. And I smile, big and wide, like I mean it. Because I do.

"Oh, no, no, no," someone whispers over my shoulder. "You're not going to get her hooked on one of *those*, are you?"

•   •   •

I don't realize how quickly my week in Erie rushed by until I'm back home. In New Jersey. By myself. Again. Listening to the second-hand on the clock in the kitchen stutter around and around, waiting for Thad to come home. Again.

It's not that I functioned so much differently in Erie. I still hardly left the house. I still—even with other people constantly standing watch and cooking every meal I ate for eight straight days—didn't nap when Blair napped, instead logging into my work e-mail account every chance I got, checking on the fallout from the big news.

Two days before we left for the wedding in Maryland, the executive editor at the magazine quit. I was next in line for his job. Or, I would have been next in line if I hadn't negotiated with the editor in chief before I went on my maternity leave to have Fridays off when I came back. All the other new moms I knew were doing it—going part-time so they could spend more time with their babies, switching jobs so they could have a more flexible schedule to spend more time with their babies, moving halfway across the country to live in a city with a lower cost of living so they could work less and spend more time with their babies. I figured I'd want to spend more time with my baby, too, so I waddled into my boss's corner office when I was seven months along, carrying a very detailed, typed, bulleted proposal for a four-day work week. My boss agreed. In theory, I was very lucky. In theory, I should have been somewhat groveling and overtly grateful, though I had no idea what any of this would mean when the baby-on-paper I was proposing to spend Fridays with was a real, live, breathing, pooping, crying baby.

Until the executive editor quit.

I immediately shot off an e-mail to my boss: "I just want you to know that, if it weren't for Blair, I would have been in your office already to campaign for this job."

And, not so immediately, my boss shot me an e-mail back: "You wouldn't have to campaign, doofus. I was going to talk to you about this once the dust settled. The ideal would be for you to realize that this mommy thing ain't no thang and that you could do it ably while working five days a week for mucho bucks."

Little did he know that I wasn't doing the mommy thang ably at home, seven days a week, for no pay. But I could do the executive editor job ably. I could definitely do that job more ably than I was doing motherhood.

And all I wanted was to do something ably. Anything. Except I didn't really want that job. It would mean more responsibility and more meetings. It would mean working well past 7 PM. I didn't want that. Not now. I didn't have the freedom for that now, no matter how ably I could have done it.

So, instead, I begin to paint our bedroom.

Our bedroom is still the same color it was when we moved in two years ago—burgundy and light pink walls accented by the sunny yellow of the attached bathroom. Painting it has been on my "List of Things to Do Before the Baby Was Even a Notion." And now, I'm bolstered by the discovery that Blair not only enjoys spending time in the Ocean Wonders Aquarium swing we finally put together last week in the family room, where it took up only slightly less space than the sectional couch and, along with the Bouncey Seat and the Gymini and the Boppy Pillow and the Exersaucer, makes me feel as if we're living inside a crayon box—but she *sleeps* in the swing. She sleeps long in it. Sometimes even an hour, during which I now can do something that makes me feel useful. Something that I can actually point to and say, "See what a good job I can do."

I start with the ceiling—white. Then the walls, a creamy brown, except for the one behind the bed, which I paint dark purple. I move the furniture myself, spackle the walls myself. When I hear Blair start crying on the monitor, I head out to the family room, release her from the swing, feed her, burp her, and then stick her back in the swing with the weird electronic tune it plays lulling her back to sleep. When the music shuts off, the house is quiet. I don't even turn on a radio. I don't want to hear a single sound. Just silence. Just me. Which is all I want, really. To be by myself for longer than the five minutes I get every day in the shower. To be alone.

Four days later, I'm finished. It's a Saturday. I'm so excited, I want to invite over all the mommies, the staff of the magazine, the mailman, and Pompadour, who is next door sweeping the construction dust off the street, to show them. Mostly, though, I want to show Thad. I want to remind him that I'm still here, that there is a wife here under all this baby fat, under all this exhaustion and this ponytail and this face that doesn't seem to remember how to smile.

He glimpsed that woman earlier this week, when he surprised me with reservations at my favorite restaurant in Philly to celebrate our two-year wedding anniversary—our first night out alone since Blair was born. We drove into the city and dropped off Blair at my friend April's row house, where I nursed Blair on the couch, praying she'd eat enough to be full for at least three hours. Thad had enveloped her in such a tight swaddle even Houdini couldn't escape it, and we hoped it would thwart any plans she had of crying for the whole time we were gone.

Even if she did, there was no way April would call us. April is the managing editor at *Philadelphia* magazine. She's used to stress. She's used to taking care of grownup writers and editors who are capable of whining far more in a three-hour stretch than infants do. Plus, April had been my friend since we started working at the magazine four years ago, randomly living next door to each other on a hidden alley in the city, in apartments with steep spiral staircases we both occasionally fell down. We walked to and from work together every day, took the same spinning class at the gym, ate at every restaurant within a fifteen-minute walk of our apartments where we always downed an entire bottle of wine no matter how adamantly we vowed, this time, not to. April knew me. And she'd visited us over the past three months. She'd witnessed me sitting on the couch, nursing Blair, and had watched my head nod and then drop, mid-sentence, as I fell asleep. She'd heard the frustration in my voice when I told her Thad had called to say he was going to the gym after work, again, for the third time in a week. April knew we needed this night.

Thad and I sat at a tiny table. He'd bought a bottle of red wine—"Italian, of course," he said, proud of himself for thinking to commemorate our honeymoon in Rome. It was the first wine I'd had since the pregnancy test. I sipped it slowly, wishing I'd checked in a book to see how much I could drink before it seeped into my breast milk. It tasted good. And it also tasted bad, like my mouth had forgotten all about red wine and had to get used to it again.

As I looked at Thad, the votive lighting his face from below, I realized I was feeling the same way about him. Like I had to get used to him again, get used to being with him *without* the baby, get used to talking with *him*, talking about *us*. We tried. But we just couldn't talk about us without talking about Blair or something we were planning because of Blair, like the barbecue I wanted to host with the mommies and their husbands, like the air conditioner we needed for her room, like the adorable little Mary Jane socks a friend sent as a gift and Blair finally fit into. I wondered if there really was an "us" left that didn't include Blair. I thought about the bedroom. I'd started painting it that morning. Maybe that would help—a new space for us.

But when I finish the bedroom on Saturday, Thad isn't home. He's supposed to be. He promised he'd be home by now. In fact, he said he'd be home two and a half hours ago. But he's not. Thad is on a grassy field, over the bridge and down the Schuylkill Expressway in Philly, playing a game of Ultimate Frisbee.

Playing.

A game.

Thad is playing a game, even though I have been home alone with Blair all day, and the day before, and every day since we drove home from Erie. Even though he called three times this past week at 5:00 as he was leaving work to let me know he would be home at 7:00 because he wanted to go to the gym. The third time, the day after our anniversary dinner, he strolled in the door at 7:45, again, and found me in the kitchen, again, with Blair in a sling, jumping up and down as she cried, again.

Staring at Thad like he had just smacked me across the jaw, I erupted: "This baby is not my job. This baby is *our* job. You are not doing your part of the job. Do you not see how much I need you to come home and relieve me? How do you not see that?"

"I'm sorry," Thad said. And he took Blair from me. And he ordered a pizza. And he picked it up. And I thought things were resolved. Because, just as I was sure he'd been wondering where the woman he'd married had run off to, I'd also been wondering where my husband had gone. Three months ago, he was standing at the foot of the delivery table making a face I'd never seen before, a face that made me forget that I'd just finished begging him to insist the doctor give me a C-section, a face so gentle and full of sincere wonder as he looked up and said, "Vicki, I can see a *head*." Two and a half months ago, he was signing his e-mails

"Thaddeus New Daddeus." Two months ago, as he was trying to lull Blair to sleep in her Pack 'n Play, I heard him over the monitor singing, "Wise men say, only fools rush in, but I can't help falling in love with you. . . . " And then, last month, he started coming home from work late. And then he started going to the gym. And then he signed up to play on an Ultimate Frisbee summer league team without talking to me about it first.

And, now, it is almost 5:00 on Saturday.

I watch the clock. I check my cell phone. Nothing. I check the answering machine on the house phone, even though I'm certain it hasn't rung. Nothing.

Before I know it, as if the legs I'm standing on belong to someone much stronger than me, I'm climbing the steps to the attic. I grab the L. L. Bean bag my friend gave us with "Blair" embroidered in hot pink on the front. I walk down the stairs and into Blair's room, where I open the top drawer of her dresser and pull out all the onesies, stuffing them in the bag. I march to the closet, yank out the dresses—none of which even fits Blair yet—and dump them, hangers and all, into the bag. I top it off with a half-empty container of diapers and an extra package of wipes, then drag it into the dining room so it's the first thing one would see when one walked through the front door. I climb back up into the attic and get a suitcase for myself. *I'm not really going to do this*, I think. But I can't stop doing it, can't stop shoving the black carry-on full of nursing tanks and those cropped pants I bought last week at Target, feeling sick and deciding it's because of the paint fumes wafting from my room. *It's going to take so long to put all this stuff away*, I think. But I keep going, lugging the suitcase on its wheels down the hall and placing it, carefully, so it's also facing the door.

Blair wakes up. She's not quite crying yet, just getting ready to. As soon as I look at her face, I start to cry. Big cries. Big tears. Because this isn't how it's supposed to be. Mommies aren't supposed to make babies sleep in swings all day. Husbands aren't supposed to desert their wives when babies are born. New moms aren't supposed to leave their husbands. Everyone is supposed to be loving this. These are supposed to be the happiest days of our lives.

I pull down the flap of my nursing tank top, and latch her on. She won't stop crying and I won't either, tears streaming down my cheeks, onto her cheeks, mixing with her tears. As I make my second lap around the dining room table, bouncing her, nursing her, the front door thumps open. There is Thad, his bare legs mapped with dirt, staring at Blair and me as if he just walked into the wrong house. He looks at the suitcase, his head tilting quizzically like the dog's does when we ask him if he wants to go for a walk, like he can't quite believe we really mean it. Thad looks at me. I look down at the suitcase, almost surprised that it's there, surprised that all of this—these past three minutes, these past three months—has come to pass.

"I'm going back to my parents' house," I say, my voice hard and firm only because I'm well aware that I'm not going anywhere, yet determined to make certain Thad believes I am, so he gets it. He needs to get it, or I will, eventually, have no choice but to go. "At least there I will have some help."

i am wrong.
i am invisible.
i am mother.

"This new you is a different but better you."

—The Girlfriend's Guide to Surviving
the First Year of Motherhood

I have just sat down in a small puddle of drool on the floor in the rec room of Sonya's house. Sonya is one of my new mommy friends I met at the movies. She has twin girls who were born a week before Blair. My other new mommy friends are here, too. Instead of going to Baby and Me, where we usually meet on Fridays and pay $4 to watch our babies lie on their backs on blankets spread out on the floor, today Sonya invited us to her house to watch our babies lie on their backs on a big quilt spread out on *her* floor. Blair isn't swaddled and is surprisingly okay with not being swaddled as she shows off her sweet green cotton romper, which I managed to iron this morning. All the mommies have commented on how cute she looks, which, of course, was the point. This morning, when she was dressed and ready, I noticed that she looked different. Her face was fuller. Her cheeks were borderline pudgy. She actually looked healthy. And baby-like. But, now, the only thing I can think when I look at those cheeks is how much I want to squeeze one of her hard white volcanoes of baby acne, much like the zits that, in reaction to the anxiety I've been toiling so desperately to hide from everyone, have exploded in constellations all over my ass.

I stand up and walk to the table where Sonya has put out "a little something"—scrambled eggs, orange juice in a glass pitcher, thin sticks of French toast warming on a portable griddle. I pour a cup of coffee and try not to hate Sonya for being so good at all this.

"I'm having such a hard time even checking my e-mail," I hear Jenn say from her perch on the couch on the other side of the room.

"Me, too," I answer, rushing back to the quilt. E-mail has been driving me crazy. All I want to do is check it to make sure I haven't missed anything important at work, and so I attempt to multitask, logging on when Blair is nursing. I sit on the couch with my laptop propped on the end table, typing with my left hand while holding Blair's head with my right.

"It's impossible," I say.

"I know," Jenn replies. "I feel like I need to call my boss and say, 'Excuse me, but I'm still on maternity leave. I'm not even getting paid right now. Stop sending me messages.'"

"No," I interrupt. "That's not what I mean . . ." I'm about to explain: *My problem isn't that e-mail is keeping me from Blair. My problem is that Blair is keeping me from e-mail.* But Sonya responds first:

"You *should* call your boss. That's just absurd."

"You totally should call him," Michelle seconds. Before I have a chance to reset my brain from how grossly I misunderstood this entire discussion, Sonya speaks again.

"I wish I could just quit my job," she says. She's a doctor at Temple University hospital. Next week, she'll be the first of us to go back to work.

I'm one breath away from laughing.

"I don't think I can do it," Sonya says. *Are you kidding?* I think. I almost say it out loud—*Are you kidding me?*—until I look around. Everyone is nodding. I think Sonya's eyes are welling up.

"I don't think I can do it either," someone says.

"Every time I think about it, I start to cry," someone else says.

"I feel like I'm betraying her or something," someone else adds, though I can't identify who, since their voices are blending in my brain in one, loud, discordant chord. How can it be that not one of these other women wants to go back to work? How can it be that I'm the only one? The *only* one? And I'm looking forward to it. I'm counting down the days: eighteen. People rarely cry at work, and when they do, they don't need me to swaddle them.

"Work is sure going to be easier than the past three months have been," I venture under my breath, as if talking to myself, though intending each and every one of them to hear each and every word, hoping someone will agree.

"Oh," sighs Meridith. She is twenty-eight, the youngest of this crew. She quit her job months before she had her son Lucas and has no intention of ever going back. She's quiet. A smiler. She refuses to leave the house when Lucas is acting even slightly cranky. And right now, she's gazing dreamily at her son's face, brushing his much-more-than-Blair hair off his forehead. "I just love Lucas too much to go back to work," she proclaims.

The room snaps silent.

I swear the other mommies have actually stopped breathing to restrain themselves from reaching over and plucking Meridith's son-adoring eyes right out of their son-adoring sockets. Did she really just say that? Is she implying what I think she's implying—that all the women in this room who are going back to work, who've been lamenting over leaving their babies, must not love their children as much as she loves hers? I lean back against the couch, waiting for the show to start. Someone's going to flip. Someone's going to discharge, likely at great volume, what everyone has got to be thinking: *What, exactly, are you trying to say, Meridith?*

Nobody speaks. I catch Jenn's eye. We both, at the same time, make the same face—raising our eyebrows and pursing our lips as if blowing out air, which translates, simply, as "Can-you-believe-her?" Jenn should say something. I know Jenn doesn't want to go back to work, and she isn't even putting Cailyn in day care since both her mother and mother-in-law live nearby and have volunteered to take care of the baby on alternating days of the week. But Jenn doesn't say anything. I think Jenn is expecting me to say something. Of course, Jenn has no idea that I'm the least likely person in this room to challenge the notion that I don't love my child enough. I already know I don't love my child enough. Moments ago, I almost stated publicly that I love e-mail more than I love my child.

So why am I so pissed at Meridith? Because I am. I'm every-cell-in-my-body-is-vibrating pissed. I want to stand up and yell at her. It feels remarkably good, not wanting to yell, but the impetus behind it. I want to defend myself. I want to defend my feelings for my child.

Which means I must have feelings for my child.

•　　•　　•

101

As I drive home from Sonya's, I'm so busy having a conversation with myself, saying out loud all the things I wanted to say to Meridith, that I barely notice the sign for the child care center. I pass this place every Friday on our way to Baby and Me. And every time I feel like I should turn in.

We started looking for day care for Blair long before she was even Blair, only because my high school friend Krysia told me to. "As early as possible," she instructed, still reeling from her frenzy to find child care after her husband, who'd agreed to be Mr. Mom to their son while Krysia worked full-time as a lawyer, decided after six months that he didn't like it. Thad and I harbored no illusions that either of us was cut out to stay at home full-time. I only half-entertained the idea because my own mother stayed home with me until I started school, took me everywhere, played with me constantly, and explained to me in great detail everything we were doing, which she swears is why I was selected for the gifted program in fourth grade. Even though I dreamed of having a gifted child, I knew I didn't have the patience to spend my days alone with one, sitting on the floor while my gifted child yelled "Again! Again!" to signal me to read *Little Ducky and Baby Quack* for the 872nd time in a row, causing my own brain to fizzle and die. Or that's how I expected it to be, since that very scene flashed in my head whenever I merged the image of "me" with the image of "stay-at-home mom."

Yet, even with Krysia's warning, I doubt I would have gotten much further than Googling local day care centers had Thad and I not decided to take one, final, kidless vacation just after Thanksgiving last year, still considering ourselves to be kidless despite my six-months-pregnant belly, which had just started demanding official maternity clothes. I suggested we go to Prague. I'd wanted to go to Prague ever since one of my high school boyfriends went there one summer to play soccer and wrote me long letters with many misspelled words about how cool Prague was.

I wasn't sure if it was possible for Thad to be more giddy than he was when our flight took off from Philadelphia International, heading to Frankfurt. But, then, two hours in, I felt something. My hand was resting on my stomach. And I felt it. I felt the baby move. I'd been feeling the baby wiggle and stretch from the inside out for about a month already, but I hadn't yet felt it from the outside in. I reached over, grabbed Thad's hand, and placed it on the spot where the baby had just kicked.

"What?" he screamed, loud because he still had his headphones on, and nervously because, so far, neither of us had paid enough attention to my growing belly to be inspired to intentionally touch it. I smiled at him. In less than thirty seconds, I felt a kick inside. Thad felt it outside. And, from that moment on, I couldn't pry his hand off my stomach until the plane touched down in Germany. We both were struck with the same realization. There was a living thing inside my body. A real, living thing. And in four months, that living thing was going to come out.

Not until I got back to work after the trip did my brain take the next logical step: And in seven months, that living thing is going to need a place to spend its days.

We had three requirements for day care. It needed to cost less than $200 a week. It needed to be flexible, since neither of us could pick up the baby before 5:45. Finally, it needed to be within a five- to ten-minute drive of our house, in the same direction as the train station, preferably on a street that had two or fewer lights and no jug-handle turns.

I found exactly what I was looking for where I least expected it—tucked at the end of the strip mall less than 2 miles from our house, just past the high school with a road behind it that was a direct shortcut to the train. It stayed open until 6:00. Whoever picked up Blair could also pick up a rotisserie chicken for dinner at the grocery store next door. It would be perfect.

I called in late to work one morning and zipped over to the day care center to take a tour. The woman at the front desk led me down the hall to the infant nap room with no windows and so many rows of cribs I could barely squeeze my belly between them.

"Do you have this many babies?" I asked, forcing myself not to envision actual human beings trying to sleep in this cave, so as not to interfere with my conviction that this place would be perfect.

"Not right now, but sometimes," she said, pushing open the door into the infant playroom. "But there is always one teacher for every five infants."

Except, apparently, for today. Today, there were two teachers in the room. One looked like she was fifteen. The other was coughing like she had tuberculosis. Four babies lay on their backs on a mat, four more crawled around a wall of cardboard blocks, and two sat in high chairs next to the refrigerator. The three smallest babies were off in the corner, rocking away in swings pumping at entirely different rhythms. Two of them were wide awake, staring straight ahead as if drugged. When I started counting kids, my tour guide swiftly grabbed my arm, pulling me to the toddler room where a teacher was holding a little boy, screaming, with blood dripping from his nose.

"Christian threw a truck at him," the teacher explained to my tour guide as she exchanged the bloody Kleenex for a clean one that she twisted into a little point and plugged into the boy's nose.

I wasn't sure why, after the tour, I was still waiting politely by the front desk for a brochure with the
lesson plans and yearly events printed at some corpo-
rate office far, far removed from truck-throwing
Christians. I just wanted to see the prices. I wanted to
know how this place compared to a $360-a-week
nanny and to the $250-a-week Jewish Community
Center 15 miles away, where I'd gone months before
while researching a magazine story and watched as
three-year-olds marched in single file from the
kitchen, where they'd baked a batch of chocolate chip
cookies, dressed in aprons they'd probably made that
morning. As I stuffed the brochure in my black work
bag and turned to leave, I heard a sharp voice prick
out of the room across the hall.

"Andrew!" the voice cackled. "Andrew! You sit down
right now! If you don't sit down right now I'm not going to let you go to kindergarten. I'm going to make
you spend another whole year *here* . . . with *meeeeeee.*"

I called Thad from the parking lot and told him
everything, furiously, like I was spitting it all over the
steering wheel.

"I will kill myself before I put my child in a place like
that," I told him, acutely aware that we'd been thinking about this all wrong, that there was much more to
this day care equation than cost and proximity and
what time the place closed. "They just ignored these
poor little babies. Jesus. They must have only been a

few months old, and they just left them all by themselves in a corner . . . sleeping all day . . . in *swings!*"

I spent that entire morning at work searching the Web for other centers, for nannies, for homes for sale in our neighborhood where my parents could move so they'd be close enough to babysit Monday through Thursday from eight to six for a nominal fee. I called the Camden County office of child services, which kept a list of people in our area who took care of kids in their homes. That seemed ideal—intimate and personal like a nanny, but social and interactive like a day care center. And when the list came in the mail, I was sold—there was one on the street north of us, and one on the street south of us. We could *walk* there.

The first woman we met looked like a stripper. I had never seen bigger, faker boobs that close in my entire life. I couldn't stop staring at them. Neither could Thad. But she was very nice and very calm, with a playroom filled with toys, and Pack 'n Plays set up in different rooms so the kids had privacy during their naps, and portable high chairs attached in a row on the island in her kitchen where she made their lunch. She charged $30 a day and she had an opening in July, which was exactly when we'd need her. That night, we called her references. We filled out paperwork. It would be perfect.

Two days later, there was a message from her on our answering machine: "Hi, Vicki and Thad. I hate to tell you this, but my husband and I just decided that we really don't want to have kids here after 5:30. Sorry." Click.

After thirteen phone calls to other home care providers in the neighborhood who either didn't call us back or had no openings or owned big black dogs that almost bit Thad's hand off, I landed on one in the next town over. She had a master's degree. She only turned on the TV during lunch. Her husband taught elementary school. They had no problem with our picking up the baby at 5:45. It would be perfect.

Three months later, right after Blair was born, she sent me an e-mail—she was pregnant and wouldn't be able to take any kids until seven months after we needed her. "Sorry," she wrote. I was certain it was a sign, some kind of supernatural message that I should quit the job I had moved to Philadelphia for, forsake the career I'd been developing for eleven years, and spend my life sitting cross-legged on the floor in the family room playing This Little Piggy Went to Market.

Then, the next morning, the phone rang. I didn't answer it because Blair had just fallen asleep in the sling wrapped around my shoulders, and I was gripping the dog's mouth shut to prevent him from barking at the four construction workers marching down our driveway, yelling to each other about how to drain the rainwater out of the foundation of the house next door. I listened as the machine recorded the message: "This is Jane from around the corner. We spoke several months ago about day care. I didn't have any room then and you asked me to put you on my waiting list. Well, a spot just opened up and . . ."

This wasn't just Jane from around the corner. It was *the* Jane from around the corner, the woman that every other day care person I spoke to mentioned as if referring to the Mary Poppins of Haddon Township. And *the* Jane was calling me. I called her back immediately—we made plans to meet that night at her house at 7:00. I couldn't wait until 7:00, though, packing Blair into the stroller, cell phone in hand. As I casually rolled back and forth in front of Jane's house, I gave Thad a play-by-play on the phone: "It's just a block and a half away! There are about 6,000 lawn ornaments in her front yard, plus two park benches, hex signs, and an aluminum windmill. I see chalk drawings on the sidewalk, and I think there's a swing set in the backyard . . . wait . . . hold on . . . there's a man coming down the driveway . . . I'll bet it's her husband. . . ." I chugged across the street and flipped around so the cell phone was hidden by my hair. "He's got some kind of Indian medicine bag around his neck. He just popped open the hood of the car . . . what do you mean, 'What kind of car?' . . . It's a green car."

When Jane opened the door at 7:00, I swore I'd met her before, like we should be picking up on a conversation that we'd started long ago. She was in her late forties or early fifties—I couldn't quite tell because her dyed red hair was spiked up with gel. The rest of her looked soft and round, with glasses and a big laugh that cuckooed right up out of her when I told her that her phone call had made my month, as did the news that she charged $35 a day and had no trouble with our pickup time. She'd been caring for kids for twelve years and couldn't wait to get her hands on Blair, whom I was bouncing in the sling, praying she wouldn't start to cry that Blair Witch cry of hers. The living room and dining room, where the four-year-old and three two-year-olds she took care of spent the day, were small, packed with toys and furniture. There was a bird in a cage on the mantle—his name was Mojo—next to photos of her three sons at prom and of little kids sitting straight and tall in school pictures.

"Oh . . . those are the kids I've sat over the years," Jane said, motioning the way my grandmother used to when pointing out my cousins and me at family reunions in the picnic grove along French Creek. And I knew then Blair was meant to be here with this woman with the clock that chimed animal sounds on the hour and the 100-square-foot sandbox in her backyard.

But now, more than two months later, driving home from Sonya's, passing the one day care center I never looked into with just eighteen days before I go back, my mind starts racing: *What if Jane's husband is a child molester? What if the kids are kept in cages and Jane's dogs pee on them?* I swerve into the center. The director takes a break from hanging decorations for the Under the Sea family party they're hosting on Sunday to show me around. There's classical music playing. There are colorful amoeba-shaped pictures taped to the walls. On the door to the infant room, there's a lesson plan for the week, which includes sign language for the word "more." I look down at Blair in her car seat hooked over my arm, her arms and legs suddenly looking rather scrawny in her cute little green romper. This kid could really use the sign for "more."

"Give it a week at Jane's," Thad says. I've called him from the parking lot, entirely expecting him to insist I walk back in and enroll her. "Blair doesn't *need* sign language. Blair needs to be hugged and carried and played with . . . "

"Played with?" I shout. "What do you mean 'PLAYED WITH'? Do you think Jane's husband is a child molester, too? Because, I swear to God, Thad, if we . . . "

"Vicki, go home *now.*"

I hang up and pull out of the parking lot.

"We'll work this out," I reassure Blair on the drive home, looking at her face in the rearview mirror. "I promise, kiddo. We have time." Even though I go back to work in two-and-a-half weeks, Blair won't start at day care until two weeks later. My parents will be there, caring for her in the meantime, until Jane returns from her family vacation at a remote cabin in the Poconos where they probably kill small game with their bare hands and impale them on branches staked around the door.

•　　•　　•

My body crumples completely in half, my head scrunched between my knees. It takes me by surprise—my reacting this way as I'm about to walk out the door, leave the house, go back to work, dressed for the first time in months in real clothes—the white cropped pants I bought at Target and a turquoise shirt gathered between my boobs so that it barely covers my beige nursing bra. Clutching my work bag, I cross through the living room to the front door, turn the knob, and then fall apart, tears dripping onto the hardwood floor. This is what I want, what I've been dreaming about for months. I'm escaping. *I have to get out of here*, I think. I have to get to the train. I have to get to my office early so I can get back in gear, water my plants, turn off the message on my phone that announces I'm on maternity leave until July 5. Until today.

I'm not supposed to be crying. This is just the trial run. The real test happens in two weeks, when I drop Blair off at Jane's for the first time, when I leave her with a total stranger, when I officially concede that being with this total stranger who doesn't even know her, much less love her, is better for my child than being with me. Right now, Blair's in the kitchen with my mom. My mom is holding her. My mom's spent more time with her than anyone other than us. She loves her. My mom probably loves her more than I love her. Blair couldn't be in better hands.

Sitting on the train, I thumb through the *Philadelphia Inquirer*. I haven't read it in three-and-a-half months despite the fact that it's been delivered to my house daily, piled with the others still in their clear plastic bags on the dining room table next to the untouched stack of parenting magazines that just kept coming and coming, though I swear I didn't subscribe to a single one. The last time I was on this train, it was winter, and I was constantly unbuttoning my coat so that people would notice that I was pregnant and give up their seat. No one ever gave up their seat. How ironic, I think, that now there are so many seats I could lie down across rows if I wanted to. How ironic that I kind of want to. How ironic that the first time I had to leave my child was the first time that I didn't want to leave her.

"Wow, you're back," the editorial assistant says as she walks by my office.

"I can't believe you're back already," says the mail guy.

"You look tired. Are you tired?" asks the assistant art director.

"Let me see a picture," says Bob, who instead of poking in his head and then walking away fast like everyone else has, as if having a baby is catchy like mono, sits down on one of my pink-and-orange chairs, visibly relieved that I'm back since he pretty much absorbed my job for the past three months. Of course, he's not single and childless like most of the staff. He's almost fifty and has two sons who are deep into puberty.

"I don't think I have any pictures," I say, leaning over to fiddle through my bag, as if a photo might magically materialize in there, despite the fact that it never even occurred to me to bring in a photo of my child. "I'm a bad mom," I say, and then immediately ask him where we are in the production schedule, if there's anything he needs me to do. I don't want to talk about Blair. I don't want to talk about anything that has to do with having Blair or with the past three months or with motherhood and how it's treating me. I just want to move forward. I want to leave all that at home. I'll deal with that there. When I'm here, I'm working. I'm the professional me. The old me.

Except that it is now 10:00. It is time to pump milk out of my boobs.

My friend Stacy was visiting the first time I used my Pump in Style breast pump, this $300 plastic contraption that sounds like Darth Vader. Stacy was moving from New Hampshire to Arizona for no reason except that she always wondered what it would be like to live in Arizona. I'd known Stacy since she was in eighth grade and I was in sixth. We met during *Snow White*—I was the witch with the poisoned apple; she was a townsperson who basically changed the sets. She was an only child, like me, and she practically lived at my house while her parents were divorcing, doing all kinds of big-sisterly things for me. She took me to see David Lee Roth in concert. She explained to me what a "blow job" was. She taught me how to drive when I was only fourteen, letting me steer around the side streets between our houses in her mom's brown Dodge Colt hatchback, pledging to each other that, from this moment on, we would officially be "sisters." We would be the maid of honor in each other's weddings. We would pluck each other's chin hairs if either one of us ever ended up in a coma. And if we ever had kids, we would be their "aunts." Blair was three weeks old when she met her "Aunt" Stacy.

"You look like a cow," Aunt Stacy proclaimed, as she knelt down in front of me, her face inches from my boob, studying how the machine sucked sprays of milk from my nipples into its clear plastic funnel connected to a bottle screwed onto the end. I felt like a cow. Though I wasn't producing nearly as much milk as a cow, barely a half-ounce spitting out that first try. I needed to start "building up a supply," according to the breastfeeding brochure the nurse gave us at the hospital, so Blair would have something to eat when I wasn't around. It seemed illogical—adding a "pumping" to my day, sometime in between the real feedings, though my real feedings were clearly inadequate since, at that point, Blair had just regained her birth weight and still looked skeletal. But a month later, when I sat in a circle at the breastfeeding support group that met every other Friday, the lactation consultant Betsy confirmed that's how boobs worked.

"The more the baby sucks, the more your body will produce," Betsy assured us, sipping coffee from a white Styrofoam cup. That rule also applied to pumping—if you pumped at the same time every day, your body would get used to it and produce more. Betsy apparently didn't understand that even though Blair had gained almost a pound since she was born, she still took over an hour to nurse, and then I had to bounce her, and then I had to hold her while she slept, and then she nursed again. How was I supposed to fit in a pumping?

"That's strange," said a woman on the other side of the circle. "I was just going to ask you if it was possible to produce too *much*. I already have 22 ounces stored in my freezer and little Lily is only four days old. What should I do?"

Leave. That was what she should do. Pick up her pink Coach diaper bag and her daughter who weighed more than she did. Because there was no telling what we were capable of, this assemblage of women who'd been distressing for the past forty-five minutes over cracked and bleeding nipples, over mastitis that gave them sweaty fevers, who were wrapping their boobs in warm cabbage leaves, who weren't pumping more than a half-ounce at a time no matter how many waterfalls they pictured in their minds, who were so worried that they were starving their babies that they came here every week to do what I'd just done: strip Blair down to her diaper, weigh her on the scale set up next to the coupon exchange, discover she only gained 2 ounces since last week, freak out, dress her, nurse her, strip her, and weigh her again to check how many ounces she'd just eaten. Breastfeeding wasn't so natural. Breastfeeding was hard. Breastfeeding hurt. Breastfeeding was probably why so many babies used to die. If this woman who clearly needed no breastfeeding support, who had lost all her baby weight because her superhuman boobs were "just melting it right off of me," if this woman didn't get her maternal ass out of this circle, she would surely be mobbed.

And, yet, I did the best I could with pumping, starting with Aunt Stacy staring at the funnel cupped over my boobs. During the following months, I fit in pumpings as often as I could—at least once a day— storing the milk in my freezer in special breast-milk baggies that could hold 5 ounces, though I rarely filled them higher than the 2-ounce line. Thad wanted to defrost a baggie every now and then to take over for a feeding at night, but I wouldn't let him. Not only did I insist, martyr-like, that feeding Blair at night was *my* job, but also I didn't want to waste the supply. I was terrified that I didn't have enough, even though I had no idea when I'd ever have the occasion to use it. Not until today, on my first day back to work, in my office, at 10:00 AM.

I hang a "Do Not Disturb" sign on my door. I lock it. I set up the pump, snake out of my shirt, flip down one flap of the nursing bra. Twenty minutes on one side. Twenty minutes on the other, as I secure the bottle in the crook of my elbow while typing an e-mail with my right hand, needing to do something productive, knowing I can't very well waste 120 minutes a day—because I have to do this at least three times— even if I'm coming in earlier. Even though no one cares what I'm doing in here. Except me. I care. I care that I can't focus, that I can't leave mommyhood at home.

I look down.

"Oh my GOD!" I shout. I pick up the bottle and hold it steady in front of my eyes to make sure I'm seeing what I think I'm seeing. The top of the milk stretches precisely across the 4-ounce line. Four ounces! *Four* ounces! This is more than I've ever pumped before! I have to show someone. I stand up, carrying the bottle like it's a $100 glass of port, and slide out from behind my desk. *Who can I show? April! I can show April! April will care!* April made it through three hours babysitting Blair on our anniversary. She can handle anything.

Except, right before I turn the knob on my office door, I picture the moment that is about to happen: me walking into April's office, me presenting April with a plastic jar filled with a vaguely yellow liquid, April reaching out and taking it. Because April trusts me, because no matter how much April can handle, she would never suspect that I'd ever hand her a bottle of anything that I'd just juiced out of my body, even if it's an impressive amount, even if it's starting to flawlessly separate with the cream sinking to the bottom and the skim rising to the top just like all the pictures in *The Womanly Art of Breastfeeding.* I walk back to my desk. I set the bottle next to my keyboard and begin to twist the pump apart, preparing to sneak down to the employee kitchen to rinse out the funnels and the tubes in the sink, hoping no one realizes what I'm

rinsing out and what is rinsing out of what I'm rinsing out.

And then, somehow, the bottle tips over.

All 4 ounces spill onto my white Target pants.
Onto my chair. Onto the carpet. Onto my keyboard,
oozing between each key. It happens too fast for me to
do anything but watch, my hands splayed in front of
me as if someone just burst into my office with a camera, my head trying to determine exactly what happened, how I let this happen, how I could possibly let
this happen. And now Blair will starve because Blair
will have nothing to eat tomorrow because Blair's
lunch is soaking in long gashes of yellow stain on my
white pants that I pray don't start to smell.

And then I remember it. The Tupperware container under the ice trays in the freezer. Filled with tiny
bags. Filled with breast-milk popsicles. The supply.

Thank God for the supply.

•   •   •

By the start of my second week back, I think I've got
everything under control—arriving at work early, not
spilling milk, leaving work early, mommying. My
body has adjusted, even though Blair is still waking
up to nurse every three hours at night, even though
every time I'm standing in the hallway, having a con-

versation with someone, I discover that I'm bouncing up and down as if there's a baby in my arms. I don't even feel sleepy during the day, or even slightly guilty when I read the postings on the listserv one of the mommies started about how everyone else is doing— "I'm hating work"; "I've been back two weeks and it's still awful." My mother flew home on Saturday and my dad is here now, keeping Blair on a routine that starts with a "front of the bus" walk outside in the morning to touch the leaves. When I get home on Monday, my dad won't give her up. He keeps holding her, keeps bouncing. After he hands me a sheet of paper listing every thing that happened all day broken down into ten-minute increments, he recounts the details of every poop, and where they walked in the neighborhood, and how she lay in her crib and gurgled while watching the mobile rotate above her head, and how she lay on her side on the play mat, staring at her reflection in the mirror velcroed to the side. I reach out to take her. He turns away.

"Noooooo," he says, jokingly.

"Really, dad," I say, reaching out again.

"No, no, noooooo," he says again, swooping Blair up into the air, beyond my grasp. My words shoot out before there's time to temper them:

"Dad. Give. Me. My. Child."

"Of course," he says, flustered as he passes Blair to me, looking kind of confused and kind of surprised and kind of scared. Of me. And the fact that I so easily snarled at him. But there's no way he could possibly be as surprised as I am. Because I can't quite believe what just happened, that I instinctually lashed out like a mama bear in the wild—all because I *wanted* to hold my child.

But, that night, my child tests me again. My child decides to start waking up every hour.

After the first couple of weeks, when I dispatched Thad to the foot of the bed to make sure Blair was still breathing, I'd moved the Pack 'n Play so it was flush against my side of the bed, making it easier for me to get to her. For the past three months, I've spent half the night inching toward the edge of the Pack 'n Play, stealthily peeking over the side so Blair won't be able to see me if she's awake, watching for movement. Every two to three hours, when I heard that hungry barking, I'd pick her up and walk down the hall to her room, where I'd nurse her in the glider rocker.

All those months, I functioned like a robot, with no emotion, only a sense of urgency based on the knowledge that there was a task to be done and I needed to do it, a task that would've been much more efficient if I'd simply moved the rocker into our bedroom. But the lavender cushions on the rocker didn't match our bedroom. And I couldn't comprehend why we would intentionally move a piece of furniture out of a room it matched into a room that it didn't, as if we would never, ever be able to move it back. I thought it would stay in our room forever because I truly believed I'd be getting up every three hours—walking across the room to the rocker that didn't match, falling asleep hunched over us both until Blair woke up, when we'd start the whole cycle again—for the rest of my life.

But then, tonight, Blair starts waking up every hour.

Three nights later, after the fourteenth person at work asks me if I've had an allergic reaction to something, I pull Blair into bed with me. I've done this before, months ago. It started innocently enough—Blair waking for her 6:00 AM feeding, me wanting to get another hour of sleep and lifting her over the edge of the Pack 'n Play into the bed, Blair latching on while I lay on my side, me not having to do anything else and really loving the "not having to do anything else" part. After a few days when I actually slept less because I was terrified I'd roll over and smother her, or Thad would, or the dog would, I started falling asleep that way. *We* started falling asleep that way. And, in the middle of the night, when Blair was quiet and calm and I could smell the lavender shampoo in her hair, I felt my heart pound. Hard. As if it was filling up with something that was thicker than blood. I looked at Blair's soft face, all shadowed by the dark and smooth with sleep, and I felt my own face soften. I felt everything about me soften—my skin, my bones, all the noise in my brain. And I felt certain then—unmistakably certain—I would not trade my life for anything.

But we stopped that. We had to, after I nonchalantly mentioned our "family bed" to Dr. Weidner at Blair's two-month appointment, and he'd asked:

"How long do you plan on doing *that?*"

"I don't know. I didn't exactly plan on doing it at all."

"You might want to consider an exit strategy. You don't want her to be sleeping with you when she's five."

What have I done? I thought. We might not have the glider rocker in our bedroom until the end of time, but we might have Blair there that long. She'll be fourteen and still sleeping with us. She'll come home from college and sleep with us. And I'll never sleep through the night again. *How could I be so stupid?* So I stopped. So I put her back in the Pack 'n Play. So I gave up the extra sleep. And the comfort. And the bonding.

But now there is no sleep at all. Now, Blair is waking up every hour. The first two nights, Thad tried to help, because, generally, Thad had been trying to be more involved since he saw my packed bags and me ready to walk out the door. When he heard Blair cry, he leapt to the Pack 'n Play, changed her diaper, swaddled her, and then positioned her body parallel to mine so she could nurse. When she wouldn't fall asleep, when she kept crying, when Thad sensed my frustration rising to "throw the baby out the window" stage, he leapt up again. He walked her. He burped her. But nothing worked. Which is why I have no choice but to bring her back into bed with me.

Blair is the only baby I know who isn't sleeping through the night. Every day on the mommy listserv there are e-mails about how Lucas slept for seven hours or how Bella slept for eight or how Joan woke up in a panic one morning because she hadn't heard a peep from Genni since she put her down the night before at nine. And all of them are sleeping in their own cribs. Then there is Blair, who freaks if we put her down at all, much less in her crib. Blair who, even though she's been sleeping with me again for two nights, still is waking up every hour. Blair who howls when her now sleepless mother pulls away because her boob has become a pacifier on which the baby relies for sleep.

"Jesus Christ!" I say, on Saturday night, when she wakes up at 2:00 AM.

"Jesus Fucking Christ," at 3:00 AM.

"What are you trying to DO TO ME?" at 4:00 AM.

"Give me a fucking BREAK," at 5:00 AM, this time so loud that it wakes the dog, who thinks it's time to get up and starts prancing around the bed, whining for his breakfast. I can't yell at him to lie down because I might disturb Blair, who at least is quiet as she's nursing, and I'm fantasizing that maybe, just maybe, she might fall asleep when she's finished. And maybe, just maybe, I will sleep.

But no.

The dog won't stop pacing.

"Levi, lie down," I whisper. He hears me, sits down beside the Pack 'n Play and stares at my face, wagging his tail, groaning, unfazed by the 11-and-a-half-pound creature glued to my chest. He barks.

"LevishutuporIwillkillyou," I say in one breath, without separating my top teeth from my bottom teeth. "Iwilltotallykillyou." Levi barks again.

"Thad," I say, twisting my head around as far as I can.

"Thad!" I say again, thinking *ThadwakeuporI-willkillyou*.

"THAD!"

"What?" Thad answers.

"Help me."

"What?"

"Now."

"What?"

"Let Levi out," I say, full voice. And the words seem to resonate as if I was standing in front of a megaphone. I wish I had a megaphone. If I had a megaphone, I would have held it up to Thad's ear three hours ago. But by this point, Levi is jumping up and down. And Blair starts crying.

"NOOOOOW!" I yell. And, at 5:16 AM, on a Saturday, we are all wide awake.

MONTH
5

see mommy run.
run, mommy, run.

*"The parents' difficulty in separating may be the
most significant hurdle in leaving a new baby.
. . . Parents will surely feel lost without the baby."*

—*Touchpoints: The Essential
Reference Guide for the Early Years*

On Monday morning, I pack two bottles of pumped
breast milk into Blair's lunchbox and fill a bag with
books and toys—all with Blair's name written on
them in black Sharpie marker—an extra onesie, a
blanket, and a light blue bib with a sailboat on it. I
also pack a list of every one of our phone numbers, a
list of the schedule I'd like Jane to follow—a morning
nap and an afternoon nap, neither of which I've been
able to persuade Blair to take—and typed instructions
outlining eleven different strategies for what to do
when Blair cries.

Blair is dressed in a seersucker turquoise-and-pink plaid jumper with a white flower appliquéd on the front. She looks cute. I'm hoping that if she looks cute enough, Jane will not tell Thad when he picks up Blair at the end of the day, "It's not going to work out." We've been wondering, all of us—my mother, my father, Thad, me, anyone who has spent extended periods of time with Blair—if Jane has ever decided that a child is just too much work.

"Do you think she ever just says, 'This kid cries too much. I don't want to deal with her'?" my mother asked before she left last week, calculating what she'll do if that happens, how she'll retire three months early, how my parents will buy a motor home and park it in our driveway, so they can live there and take care of Blair during the day.

I make the drop-off quick. I carry Blair in her car seat up the front steps, past the aluminum windmill, past the blue wooden bird staked in the ground holding a sign that says "Hi." I walk through the door. I hand Blair to Jane. I've been preparing for this moment, preparing to feel selfish for choosing not to stay home with her, choosing to leave her with this strange woman, choosing to put my needs over hers. *I'm totally going to lose it*, I think. *I gotta get out of here.*

I lean down and kiss Blair on the forehead, thankful that she's acting so mellow. Three two-year-old girls run in and out of the door of a plastic toy garden set up in front of Jane's fireplace. The four-year-old explains to me how she's going to help Miss Jane take care of Blair. It all plays out like a silent movie in front of my eyes. I'm going to cry—everyone cries when they drop their baby off at day care for the first time— but I don't want Blair to see me cry. I want her to think this is normal. So I go. Close the door behind me. Walk down the path to the minivan.

And I sit there.

And I wait.

And nothing happens, nothing except this sensation of weightlessness, like air's being pumped out of my body through my eyes. I feel like I've been let out of prison. Like I can breathe. And the fact that I feel so relieved makes me feel more selfish than I ever could have imagined feeling. So, on my way to the train station, I force myself to cry. Just so I can tell the mommies I did, so I can someday tell Blair I did: "I cried when I dropped you off at day care the first time."

When I get to work, there are already e-mails in my inbox from the mommies. "How are you feeling?" "How did it go?"

I write the same thing to all of them: "I cried."

The lifestyle editor stops by my office. She had her daughter a year before Blair was born and is about twenty-six minutes away from having her second. "How was it?" she asks.

"I cried," I say, quickly and firmly. *I cried. Okay? And, no, I still don't have any pictures. I forgot.*

Thad calls.

"Yeah, it was hard," I say. "Yeah, I cried."

"I know it was hard," he says, softly.

"I gotta go," I snap back and hang up fast. I know Thad feels bad for me. He thinks my clipped tone comes from my need to appear strong, to be tough and resilient. But it's actually the opposite; it's actually my need to appear emotional and vulnerable that's making me so annoyed right now—with him, with the lifestyle editor, with the mommies, with anyone else who dares to ask me how this morning went. I'm upset because people are asking me if I'm upset about something I'm not upset about, which makes me upset. And makes me lie. Not technically. Because I *did* cry. And the truth wouldn't be such a horrible thing to admit at my job, where I've been MIA for almost four months, because the truth would be strategic here. *I'm so glad I'm back. I missed you all terribly, certainly more than I'm missing Blair right now.* Basically, I'm just lying to myself. And the more I lie, the more I start to believe it. And isn't that what I really want? I want all the lies I'm telling to be true. I want to *want* to be with Blair. I want to miss her. I want to cry when I think about her smell.

April strolls into my office and props herself up on my credenza.

"How was it?" she asks. Ever since I started to try to get pregnant and, over lunch one day, gave April a primer on how to tell when you're ovulating, which included a very detailed description of the ever-changing consistency of cervical fluid, April began keeping a list. She called it "Reasons Why I Will Never Have a Baby," and she added to it, periodically, as I shared with her the many mysteries uncovered during my pregnancy. Number 14: Leaking nipples. Number 72: Kegel exercises. Number 112: The term "bloody show." Number 136: The term "crowning." Number 154: The likelihood of pooping during delivery. "I'm very anti-pooping on a doctor," she explained as we drove to New York City for the evening, eleven days before my water broke, when I was approximately the size of a double-wide, just to see Josh Lucas play the part of the Gentleman Caller in *The Glass Menagerie* on Broadway because, ever since we saw him in *Sweet Home Alabama*, we were so obsessed that we each had a photo of him looking very rugged pinned to the bulletin boards in our offices. And now I'm about to give her another thing for her list, because she is the only person who I think might possibly understand. At least about day care this morning.

"It was kind of weird," I whisper to her. "I was all ready to burst into tears when I dropped her off, and then, I didn't. And I felt so bad that I didn't feel bad that I forced myself to cry on the drive to the train. So

I could say I cried. So I could tell Blair, in like sixteen years, that I cried when I dropped her off at day care."

"You forced yourself to cry?" April asks.

"Yeah."

"So you could someday tell Blair that you cried?"

"Yeah."

April starts to laugh.

I start to laugh. The words weren't funny when I said them. But hearing April repeat them back to me, listening to how my mind is processing things, amazes me, as if the old me is hearing the new me talk for the first time. Because it does, actually, sound funny. I, actually, sound funny—the me, here on the thirty-sixth floor with the first draft of the Best Schools package on my desk that will occupy twelve pages in a glossy magazine that 140,000-plus people will read, the me that was pulled into a meeting this morning with two other editors to map out next month's issue. The me worrying that my five-month-old daughter—who, just three days ago, rolled over for the first time as she appeared to struggle to get a clearer view of Matt Lauer on TV, inspiring Thad and me to simultaneously flip open our cell phones and call our parents with the news that "Blair rolled over!"—might care that I didn't cry the first time I dropped her off at day care. That anyone might care. Other than me. But that story might be funny here at the office—the "making myself cry" part. And the story about the time I discovered poop in her hair when Blair and I were strolling through Target. And me calling Blair "The Devil Child." And "Linda Blair." That could be funny. Here. I could talk about those things here, where meetings often devolved into competitions over who could be the most quick-witted, where the editor actually called the Philadelphia chief of police to fingerprint the staff when someone kidnapped his 3-foot-high singing James Brown doll. Bad mommy stories would kill here. And I could, simultaneously, purge them. I could say them out loud, which might make them go away. Or, at least, absolve me of them.

I'm feeling rather hopeful about all this until I'm on the train on the way home, reading the *Inquirer* that I'd stuffed in my bag this morning when I realized that the only thing my mind was capable of after four hours of sleep was looking out the window, counting the prisoners in the yard as we passed over the Camden jail. But I see it now—the story, in the New Jersey section, barely two hundred words long, about an eighteen-year-old who'd been arrested the day before for shaking his three-month-old daughter to death.

I turn the page, hoping to halt all the thoughts that are ricocheting through my mind. But it doesn't work. I can't stop it, can't stop imagining how confused that baby must have felt, wondering what was happening to her, wondering why she was hurting so much. And I really can't stop thinking about that boy.

That father. Because I understand. Because I have been there. I've felt my hands squeeze too tight on Blair's chest. I've felt the vibration in my shoulders, felt it inching down, past my elbows, toward my wrists, my nose flaring, my heart racing, my mind stepping in at the last second like an alarm.

No.

Stop.

But that mind, my mind, has fifteen years on that poor kid in the paper, fifteen years of life and experience, fifteen years of experimenting with thresholds of control. But this kid? What skills does he have when I, at thirty-three, have so little myself? What does he know? What will he know now, and forever from now, except the fact that he killed his child?

This story isn't funny. No matter how I spin it. No matter whom I tell it to. It will never be funny.

And so, I decide not to tell it to anyone.

I drive to Jane's, since Thad has a late meeting and can't pick Blair up. I walk into the living room. Blair is lying in Jane's arms, all swaddled and sleeping.

"You win the award," Jane says.

"What?" I say, unfastening the straps on the baby carrier.

"You get a gold star! In all my years of doing this, you're the only mom who didn't call once during her baby's first day. The *only* one! Good for *you!*"

● ● ●

"Vicki, just turn off the monitor!" Thad says. We are in bed. It is 11:15 at night. His light is on. My light is off. I am lying on my stomach with my arms folded over my ears, hoping to drown out the sound. I am chanting: "Oh my God. Oh my GOD!"

Twenty-two minutes ago, we put Blair to sleep in her crib in her room for the first time. We flicked on the white-noise machine we bought after the long drive to Erie three months ago when the constant hum of the air conditioning knocked her out. We made sure the blinds were closed as tightly as possible, that the changing-color nightlight was plugged in. We turned on the mobile at the highest setting so that it would play the Second Movement from Beethoven's Piano Sonata in E Minor, over and over and over. The crib was empty—not a stuffed animal, not a blanket, not a thing that could smother her—save for this sack of a baby, swaddled so much she looked twice her size, propped on an inclined foam cushion we bought because it promised not only to keep her from rolling over but also to protect her from choking on her own vomit, should she spit up, which fortunately was the one thing, besides pooping, that Blair did not frequently do.

Eleven seconds after we closed the door to her room, Blair began to cry. Though I'd listened to Blair cry thousands of times before, this time was especially difficult, because even if I wanted to, even if I thought

I'd magically been zapped with baby-whispering powers, I couldn't go in and even try to comfort her. That was the point of "crying it out," which we were trying for the first time tonight—literally letting her cry for however long it took until she fell asleep.

We're letting Blair "cry it out" because, last week, Nancy and her husband let Bella "cry it out" after Bella started, suddenly, waking up in the middle of the night. Bella was the first one. Then Amy's daughter Madison. Then Meridith's son Lucas, who was waking up three or four times a night.

"I'm working on choppy hours of sleep and it's really hurting my ability to function," Meridith wrote from home on the mommy listserv last week, during the day, while I was at work.

I responded, privately, to Jenn: "I feel soooo bad that Meridith is 'working on choppy hours of sleep.' . . . Um . . . are you KIDDING me?"

And Jenn responded, privately, to me: "I have no sympathy for anyone who has the slightest possibility of napping during the day."

I had no sympathy either, especially since Lucas had been sleeping through the night for months. So had all the other kids. Except Blair. Which means all the other mommies had been sleeping through the night for months. Except me. And now what? Was Blair just going to skip over the "sleep through the night" stage? Was she just going to proceed directly to this new "waking up for no obvious reason" stage? Was I never, ever going to sleep again? Didn't people who never sleep get ill? Didn't they develop weird neurological disorders? And polyps on their brains? Didn't they die? Was I going to die?

And then, yesterday, I got an e-mail from Nancy.

"Last night she slept thru!" she wrote.

When I got home from work, I pored through the baby books to find out exactly how we were supposed to do this "crying it out" thing. Every book outlined a different strategy. We could "Ferberize" her by going in after five minutes, then after ten, then after fifteen, patting her back to let her know we hadn't jumped in the car and sped to Atlantic City where we planned to assume new identities managing a funnel cake shop, leaving her to starve, all alone, in this lacquered white cage. Except, *Healthy Sleep Habits, Happy Child* warned that patting interferes "enormously with learning to fall asleep unassisted," that ignoring all crying works best for fussy babies like Blair. But, then, Dr. Sears thought crying it out went "against a mother's basic biology." He thought that the "baby loses trust" in the mother and this mistrust "will carry over into other aspects of their relationship," which I assumed meant that Blair's first words would be "I hate you, Mommy," and then she would immediately have every part of her body that sticks out pierced. Instead, Dr. Sears said I should "lay on hands." I should "warm the bed sheets." I should "cuddle up." Cuddle up? Cuddling up was what got me into this wake-up-every-hour mess in the first place.

"Okay," Thad announced when he came home from the gym. "We'll 'cry it out.' We'll do it tonight."

"But Dr. Sears says it's inhumane," I said, as I picked up *The Baby Book* from the stack on the coffee table and flipped to the page I'd dog-eared an hour before.

"Didn't you just read me a paragraph from another book that said 'crying it out' was best for babies who cry a lot?"

"Yeah," I answered, flipping to another page I'd marked. "But what if she thinks we've abandoned her? Because that's what Dr. Sears says. He says that . . . "

"Vicki, you're driving me crazy."

"What?"

"Why don't you just pick one?"

"Why don't *I* just pick *one*?" I heard the anger in my stomach cough out when I said the word "one," as if the word were on fire. *Calm down*, I thought to myself. *Breathe*. Except that I knew I was already about thirteen giant steps beyond breathing.

"Yeah, pick *one*."

"How do *I* just pick one?" I said louder, since all my words were on fire now. I didn't have the energy to be diplomatic with this man who seemed to have suddenly forgotten all the conversations we'd had about how frustrated I was by the books, about how he wasn't helping enough, about how tired I was of trying to figure everything out by myself.

"I don't know how to pick," Thad answered, his words on fire now, too.

"Clearly," I said.

"That's not fair."

"You bet your ass that's not fair." I was standing inches in front of Thad in front of the stove. I was waving the pointer finger of my right hand, feeling a strong urge to poke him in the eye with it. Until I looked down. And he looked down. At the same time, we noticed Blair, who was sitting in his arms, in the "front of the bus." Blair was crying. Red and crying. And we both knew it had nothing to do with her colic or the demon living inside her skull or whatever it was that was making her so unhappy so much of the time. She was crying because we were yelling. I expected to feel a rush of shame. I expected to cool down instantly. But I didn't. And I didn't care. All I could think was, *Well I guess she's going to have to get used to this.*

"Anyway, I *told* you what I thought," Thad whispered in an exaggeratedly pleasant tone, usually reserved for addressing puppies.

"You did not," I said, mimicking his pitch.

"I did so. I told you we should cry it out."

"You want to cry it out?"

"I want to cry it out."

"Then we'll cry it out."

Blair has been crying it out for twenty-two minutes when I throw the comforter off and start to pace—down the hall to the door to her room and back to the bed. It doesn't seem like it's been twenty-two minutes. It seems like it's been three hours. Of crying. Constant crying. Amplified by the baby monitor stationed on my nightstand. I walk back down to her door. I stand there. I can't do anything. I'm not supposed to do anything. I'm not good at not doing anything. Not that I've been in control of much for the past five months. Not that I've done a particularly good job of taking control, except for pretending that I was in control. But this is *choosing* to give up control, which feels to me, as I stand by a door that I'm not allowed to open, like choosing to give up food, to give up the toes on my left foot.

I walk back to our bedroom. I shut off the monitor. For a second, it's quiet. Then I hear Blair, her tinny voice echoing down the hall. Over the air conditioner. Over the fan spinning above me. Far away. Farther away than her cries have ever sounded to me, like they're down a long tunnel, in another house. I turn the monitor back on. I should listen. If I'm going to make her go through this, if I'm going to put her in a crib she has never slept in before, shut the door, and let her cry, I'm going to listen to her crying. That's the least I can do, while she may or may not be suffering in there, while this may or may not be inhumane. I look at the clock—twenty-six minutes.

"I can't stand this," I say to Thad, as I walk around the bed and sit down on the edge of his side. He's not sleeping. He's staring at the window. His eyes are wide as if he's expecting someone to crash through it.

"I can't either," he says, not looking at me. "How long are we supposed to wait?"

"An hour."

"An *hour?*"

"Well, some books say we shouldn't go in until morning."

"Until *morning?* What if she doesn't stop crying?"

I grab fistfuls of the comforter, squeezing so tightly that my fingernails dig right through the fabric and into the palms of my hands. I hold on as if it's the only chance I have to restrain myself. Because my body is shaking. My body, my cells, my marrow— my "basic biology"—wants to drag me toward the door down the hall. My body wants to burst into Blair's room, to rescue her. I'm holding on to the comforter, wondering where this nurturing instinct is coming from. Wondering where it's been. And, now that I have it, now that it's tuned in loud and clear, I'm choosing to ignore it and let her cry.

The crying stops. Abruptly. I turn around and see Thad, on his knees on the floor on my side of the bed, pulling the monitor plug out of the wall.

"What are you doing?" I ask.

"I'm going to take this. I'm going to sleep in the guest room. It'll be easier for me to handle this."

"No, Thad," I protest, crawling across the bed, reaching to take the monitor from his hands. "We should do this together."

"You need to sleep," he says, flicking off the light. I lie there, on my stomach, bisecting the bed. I love him for doing this, for finally getting it, for finally understanding that I can't do this alone. But I also hate him for doing this, for letting me off the hook. I keep listening, curled up under the covers, my knees pulled against my chest, a tear slipping down my cheek that embarrasses me, even though I'm all alone. I watch the clock—12:07, 12:46, 1:22.

I startle awake in the middle of a dream in which I'm falling from the top of a tower in the woods. There's light squeaking in between the mini blinds. *Blair is dead.* I move down the hallway as if I'm rolling on wheels. I crash through her door, to the crib, where her tiny body is no longer wedged in her special sleeping pillow but lying perpendicular to it, on her stomach where she's not supposed to be. Her hands are fisted against her chin; her swaddle is completely unraveled. She is sleeping. Or she is dead. I can't tell which, and the second seems far more likely than the first. I reach down, stretch my pointer finger under her nose. There is nothing. There is absolutely nothing. Except that, there is. So gentle and warm that my skin is too tough to feel it right away. My skin needs to get used to it—her breath.

I want to know what happened. I want to wake Thad up. But my legs are heavy. My eyelids are heavy. Every part of me is heavy, stalking for more sleep. I look at the clock in Blair's room. It is 5:21. I may have slept for four hours. I haven't slept for four hours in a row in almost six months. But my body isn't grateful. It's greedy, stiffer and slower than it's been in the mornings during the past couple of weeks, when I've slept only minutes at a stretch. I limp back down the hall to my bedroom, grabbing a towel from the linen closet that I tuck under my shirt, already soaked with milk leaking from my boobs that are aching as if they've been stretched too far. I slide into bed, only noticing now that the sheets are soaked, too.

I hear the very first notes of Blair's cry. I may have been lying there for two minutes or for two hours—I don't know—but before I can figure it out, I'm standing above her, lifting her out of the crib. When she sees my face, she starts to grunt.

"Oh, pootie, I'll bet you're hungry," I say, using the name we called her when she was inside me, before we knew if she was a boy or a girl, before we knew that she actually would come out and be here and not ever go away. I sit down on the glider rocker, wrapping us both in the beige blanket Thad's mother knitted for me for Christmas last year. As soon as she latches onto my left breast, the right one starts to drip. Thad is standing in the doorway. He doesn't look tired.

"When did she fall asleep?" I ask.

"I'm not sure."

"When did she wake up the first time?"

"I don't know. Maybe around 2:00?"

"Maybe? Around 2:00?"

That night, Thad sleeps in the guest bedroom again. Blair's night is pretty much the same—waking up twice for about fifteen minutes each time. The next night, she wakes up twice but stays awake for less time. The third night, Thad doesn't remember her waking up at all. The fourth night, she cries for ten minutes when we put her down and that, he is sure, is all.

I do not wake up—only once, during the third night, when I run down to check on her, certain that she's dead, again, wondering if there will ever be another night in my life when I don't question, at least once, whether Blair is still alive. But her room is quiet. She is quiet. She did it. *We* did it.

Something we did worked.

I half-expect someone at work to bake me a cake to celebrate how alert I suddenly am. Even though I still have months of sleep to catch up on, I'm sitting in a senior staff meeting on the morning after Cry It Out Night Number Three, forming actual words, completing actual sentences, and remembering what articles are in the pipeline instead of asking, as I have been week after week, about the same stories each time, "Now, what's that New Hope story again? Now, remind me, why do we care about the casinos in Fishtown?" But no one notices. No one even comments about how the color has returned to my face or about how my voice is no longer in Lauren Bacall's range. Other than that, though, what has there been for them to notice? How would they know anything is different when I've been adamant about proving to them that nothing is?

But something is different. And it's not just the sleep. But the sleep helps me see it, makes it possible for me to recognize that something happened three nights ago. Something that transported me back to the beginning, when I was certain I couldn't love Thad any more than I did then, when I told my mother after my first sleepless night, "I think I'm going to like being a mom." That was when everything was the way I'd expected it to be—when I felt what I thought was maternal bliss, when Thad was so excited, so present, because Blair was so new. Everything was so new. I hadn't felt any of that in so long, not until I sat listening to Blair cry, feeling an urge that was beyond my understanding to go in and protect her the way a mother is supposed to, witnessing Thad step in to protect both of us the way a father is

supposed to. Maybe it wasn't that I didn't have it—
that love, that capability for love. Maybe it just
needed time to germinate before it would poke
through the ground.

An icon starts bouncing on the toolbar on the bottom of my computer. I have new e-mail. I click into
the system and see Thad's name, in bold, at the top
of the list. He's written only one line in the body: "I
just found these on my computer. . . . " There are three
black ultrasound photos. They were taken almost exactly eleven months ago, in September, our first look
at the creature that we'd made that was growing inside me somewhere. It barely weighed anything at all.
It was smaller than a fig. But there was a head. And a
body. And a hand, the tips of all five fingers pointing
forward, as if it were trying to wave.

●   ●   ●

I've just arrived at the *Philadelphia* magazine staff
pool party, held every August at my boss's parents'
house because they have a pool. I'm in the powder
room, just off the kitchen, changing into my bathing
suit, standing on the toilet to get a clearer view of myself in the mirror above the sink, as if this view will be
less disturbing than the view of me in my bathroom at
home last night. As if any view of myself at all is go-

ing to make me feel better about being one-layer-of-spandex-away-from-naked in front of the people I work with every day.

I bought this bathing suit two weeks ago, the night before two of the mommies met Blair and me on Friday afternoon at the community pool a few blocks from our house. The marketing company Jenn works for gives Friday afternoons off in the summer. Nancy cut her maternity leave short in exchange for a part-time schedule for a few months. I'd been counseling them both over e-mail, offering them talking points to present to their bosses for negotiating to have Fridays off permanently. They both wanted it—Jenn because she was having a really hard time being away from Cailyn and Nancy because she was having a really hard time being away from the mommies. I think I wanted them to have Fridays off more than they did. I didn't know what to do on my Fridays without them. What do mothers *do* with non-crawling, non-speaking, non-pincer-gripping infants? Walk around the mall? Stand at a playground and watch other people's children spin down the curly slide?

There had to be more than going to Baby and Me, sitting on a blanket, and eating a cinnamon-raisin bagel with light cream cheese. That no longer felt adequate, anyway, particularly when I took Fridays off—and had taken a pretty sizable pay cut to take Fridays off—in order to spend quality time with my child.

Good mothers did more than eat bagels. Good mothers went to the zoo and the aquarium. Good mothers signed their children up for music classes and swimming lessons and horseback riding. Good mothers took their children into the light of day, let them breathe fresh air, dangled their toes in a pool. But good mothers who invited other mothers to go to pools with them also needed a bathing suit in which to do it since the bikinis in that mother's dresser drawer no longer covered even a small fraction of the left edge of that mother's belly button.

At Kohl's, there were three styles to chose from, all of them well-suited for a water aerobics class at a senior center. I picked a black one cut high on the chest and low on the thighs, with a built-in bra that had points in the cups, decorated in multicolored flowers the size of large grapefruits. I decided the flowers looked impressionistic. Plus, the spandex held in my gut. Not that anyone besides me was looking anymore.

Earlier that week, as I walked from the train to my office, I spied a group of construction workers sitting on the sidewalk up ahead. As always, I pretended I didn't see them, all the while straining my peripheral vision so much that my right eyeball felt like it was going to seize in a cramp. I walked by the old guys with the white buzz cuts. No reaction. I walked by the cute dark-haired kid with the tattoos. Nothing. I walked by the buff one with the silver bolt in his tongue. Nada. My body kept on walking, but my saucy inner vixen fell to her knees right there on that sidewalk, her face straining up to the heavens, her fists trembling in the air, her voice growling, "For the love of Jesus, what has *happened* to me?"

Until I started looking pregnant, I got my fair share of up-and-down glances, a little whistle here, a little "Mornin' doll" there—moments that I outwardly scoffed at with a sniff of Women's Studies 101 annoyance and inwardly, secretly, celebrated with a little happy dance and the first verse of "I Feel Pretty." Now that I was no longer with child, I expected things—so many things—to return to the way they were.

But, it appeared that I'd become invisible to construction workers. I'd crossed the Line. I'd evolved. I was now a "Mom." How could they tell that I'd had a baby? That pregnancy gave me back fat? And hair in places where hair should not be? How did they not see the one positive physical change? These massive, fabulous, first-time-in-my-life-bigger-than-an-A-cup nursing boobs, boobs that now required a bathing suit with a built-in, pointy-cupped bra to contain them as I thundered over to the kiddie area at the community pool with Blair on my hip?

I crossed my legs Indian-style with Blair propped on my thighs. We were sitting at the very edge of the pool, where the floor started to slope toward the deeper, two-foot water where older, larger children were splashing too much. In front of us, arches of water shot up from holes in the bottom of the pool, which I hoped would distract Blair so she didn't realize that the half-inch of water I was about to dunk her butt in was just a few degrees away from ice.

Blair was not wearing a hat. Bella and Cailyn were wearing hats. And swimmy diapers. We didn't have either. It never occurred to me that we would need either. I didn't even know that swimmy diapers existed, or precisely what they did that regular diapers didn't do. Blair *was* wearing a very chic light-blue-and-yellow bathing suit. She was also wearing a gallon of 50-block sunscreen, which we owned only because my friend Krysia included it in her baby shower gift that she titled "All the Things You Should Have Registered for but Didn't." Most of the sunscreen was on Blair's head since her peach fuzz hair had no effect in shielding her semi-transparent scalp from the sun. Unfortunately, the gallon of sunscreen, which had the consistency of toothpaste, shaded Blair's skin a ghostly white, so she looked paler than usual. The other mothers with their bags and bags of toys, each piece meticulously marked with their last names, were surely whispering behind their liters of Evian. *Can you believe she brought that sick baby to the pool? Is she trying to give that poor child pneumonia? And, by the way, my grandmother has that bathing suit.*

A baby started to wail. Instinctively, I looked down at my baby. It had to be my baby. It was always my baby. But Blair was not wailing. For once. The wailing was not coming from the throat of my child. My child was watching the sprays of water, her head darting whenever a child ran past, like she was seconds away from standing up and chasing him. Her hands were clutched around my thumbs. Little bubbles of spit popped in the corners of her mouth. And, when I leaned in closer, I could hear her humming. She was enjoying this. The pool. The water. Sitting on my lap in the pool. In the water.

I'd been wondering if it was true—all the notes that Jane had been writing on the logs I'd asked her to keep, which she tucked into Blair's lunchbox at the end of the day. That Blair had been sleeping, unswaddled, in the Pack 'n Play. That she'd been sitting, contentedly, in the Exersaucer. That "she was very chatty and smiled a lot today." That "she's a little doll." That wasn't the Blair I knew. The Blair I knew was never chatty. She never smiled. Or she rarely smiled. Or maybe I was trying so hard to get her to stop crying that I didn't notice her smiling. I didn't see how happy she was when the swaddling worked, when the bouncing worked, when she calmed down, because I was already preparing for the next fit. Because I was living meltdown to meltdown, oblivious to what transpired in between.

Like humming, in the water, at the pool.

This would be so much easier if Blair were here, I think now as I climb down off the toilet in my boss's parents' powder room and pull my black beach cover-up over my head, hoping the fringe dangling from the hem will divert attention from, basically, everywhere else. Blair would have been perfect camo, especially now that she's sleeping straight through the night, from 10:00 to 7:00, which means I'm sleeping through the night, which means we're both more fun to be around. Blair would have been the center of attention of this party, splashing around in her little bathing suit, sticking out her tongue since she just discovered her tongue and the fact that she can stick it out whenever she wants to, which is constantly, and makes Thad and me laugh since we never considered how funny tongues could be. Last week, I mentioned to my boss that I might bring Blair to the party. He looked at me as if I'd just suggested I bring Osama Bin Laden.

Not that I had a choice. The pool party was mandatory. My boss, who is forty-three years old and wears custom-made $700 suits, said so: "The staff pool party at my parents' house is mandatory." Of course, my boss is a man who, on certain mornings, upon the arrival of each employee, will remove his suit coat, his shirt, his tie, and his undershirt so we can stand right up close to his hairy chest and best examine the violent bruising on his arm where, the night before, his orthopedist "scraped" him to cure his tennis elbow. He doesn't think there is anything odd about this. Nor does he think there is anything odd about a mandatory staff pool party, at his parents' house, with their electronic frog along the walkway that croaks when you walk past it, and the talking George Bush statue on the picnic table, and the stuffed dogs that sway and sing, "I Got You Babe." Not to mention the annual game of pool basketball when staff members inevitably come in full contact with each other and when the editorial assistant's strapless bikini top slides down at least once.

I walk through my boss's parents' kitchen, briefly saying hello to my boss's parents, who are sitting at the table, sipping iced tea, flipping pages in a huge book that looks like it may be an original copy of the Gutenberg Bible. The thick, black pages are chipping off along the edges. The tape holding the random newspaper articles in place has yellowed, some strips falling off. I realize what it is: the scrapbook of my boss's life. Black-and-white pictures. Crayon scribbles. The first article he ever wrote.

"Did you give me your order? Burger? Hot dog?" his dad asks.

"Hot dog, please. And thanks again for doing this. It's always such a blast," I say quickly, waking myself from the trance of the scrapbook and the fact that it's lying here, in public, for all to see, and the fact that my boss knows it's here and is allowing it to stay here, like this is normal, like I will be doing this someday with Blair's baby book, if I ever get my maternal act together to fill in a single line on a single page in Blair's baby book.

I swing open the screen door as if the quicker I do things, the quicker this will be over. Though it's not the pool party that needs to be over for me. It's the moment, the one that woke me up at 4:52 this morning, a time I hadn't seen glaring from my clock since Blair had been sleeping through the night. I couldn't convince myself to fall back to sleep. I just lay there, psyching myself up that it would be okay, that I could wear this bathing suit in front of people who did not push a child out of their bodies five months ago, including an intern who asked me recently, "After you have the baby, what happens to all that extra skin on your stomach?" *You don't need to hide your body*, I assured myself.

Of course, I couldn't really hide it. The other new-mom stuff? I could hide that. I could hide the fact that I didn't know who I was anymore. I could hide the frustration with Thad and the ambivalence toward Blair and the resentment I felt a few mornings ago when I got out of the shower and caught a glimpse of my naked body in the mirror and yelled, "Good Lord, noooooooo!" But I couldn't hide the body itself. No, the body, which now looked suspiciously like my mother's body, was a concrete reminder that I'd changed into this new person, this person I didn't particularly like, this person I wanted to go away but who didn't seem to be going anywhere. *No one's going to care,* I thought as I lay in bed. *No one's going to look.* Except they were going to look. Because I'd been coming to this pool party for three years and I'd looked. I knew who had eczema. I knew who had the biggest boobs. I knew who had unnaturally long underarm hair.

When I step out onto the concrete patio, it's immediately encouraging to me that no one shouts out the word "Whale!" I beeline to the first person I see—my friend Sabrina, a contributing writer at the magazine, standing under the umbrella table, dipping a corn chip into a bowl of salsa while holding, with her other hand, one of the screened domes with the wicker butterfly handles that are protecting all the hors d'oeuvres from flies. Sabrina had a baby four months before I had Blair. Unfortunately, Sabrina looks like she never had a baby. In fact, Sabrina looks like she's twenty-two years old, not a bubble of fat poking over the low-cut waist of her bathing suit bottom, no tiny folds of weird wrinkled skin above her bellybutton, no evidence of a paunch—past or present—peeking out from under the top with the underwire buttressing her cleavage, far too perky for a woman who just stopped nursing her child, whose boobs should be dangling somewhere in the vicinity of her knees.

"Sabrina! My God! You look great," I say, wishing I'd worn the brace I'd gotten from the doctor last month to control the tendonitis in my left wrist, brought on from having to hold Blair so much. The brace is big and impressive, bigger and more impressive than it needs to be—an ideal distraction at a moment like this.

"Thanks," she says. "So do you." She is lying. If I'd been wearing the brace, she would have said, "What happened?" and we both would have been spared these awkward seconds of silence, when the only thing I can think to say is, "You're lying." Even so, I still need to do this. I still need to convince myself that I'm okay with this person I am now, 15 extra pounds and all, skin tags and all, butt zits and all. I reach down, grab hold of the fringe, and lift up. With the cover-up crinkled in my hand, I stand there, jutting back my shoulders, forcing my spine into such a straight and confident posture that it hurts. I walk around the pool to the cooler, walking like I walk around the thirty-sixth floor all day long, every day, in a black spandex grandma bathing suit with enormous flowers that from far away probably look like gunshot wounds. No one is gasping. No one is averting their eyes in horror. No one is even looking at me. No one cares. I suddenly feel foolish for trying to hide it in the first place, all of it—my body, my dark circles, my child. They've known all along that I've changed. They just don't care. I'm the one who cares.

Just then, my boss's father appears, waving us all toward the umbrella table. I'm halfway there when I realize he is holding a camera.

"Group shot," he says.

"What?" I don't say it—someone else does.

"Get together, over here, on the bench."

I sit down on the bench. I relax my arms and lean back in the seat. I direct others to sit in front of me, because even though I know this photo will only be displayed in my boss's scrapbook, I'd rather be as hidden as possible, for posterity's sake. He clicks the photo. Done. Finished. A few minutes later, he comes back outside to fire up the grill. But before he does, he places a few pieces of paper on the umbrella table. The photo. Printed on his computer. And not just one copy. Ten copies. At least ten.

I stare at them as if they were a car accident. If it weren't for the splotches of bright flowers, I wouldn't have recognized myself at all.

MONTH
6

mothers of invention

"Baby and mother . . . bring out
the best in each other."
—*The Baby Book*

It's Friday morning, and it's raining, which is why I head over to Baby and Me for the first time in weeks. As usual, I'm late. When I spot my circle of mommies spread out in the corner of the playroom, they're all laughing. Hard. I park my stroller, pull out the car seat with Blair in it, and hopscotch over the other mommy cliques camped all over the floor.

"What?" I say when I get to the corner. They're all still laughing, and I kind of want them to be quiet because Blair is sleeping and looking really peaceful and pretty. I want them to notice. "What's so funny?"

"I almost killed Bella last night," Nancy says, shaking her head. She sucks in a breath, laying Bella down on her back so she can use her hands for better punctuation. "So I have that papasan—that bouncy-seat-thing—sitting on the coffee table. And Bella is in it. And it's in vibrate mode. And she's not strapped in because I never strap her in. And I'm sitting there. And the thing just vibrates right off the table! And . . ." Nancy pauses because she's laughing again. "And Bella flips over the top of it. Like, right over the top and onto the floor. She was fine. Just fine. But the thing vibrated . . . off the *table!*"

I laugh. Even though I can't quite understand why she had the papasan on the coffee table in the first place. Or why she hadn't strapped Bella in—which is something I always do, because the directions say to always strap the baby in, and by strapping Blair in, I know for sure that I'm doing one thing I'm supposed to be doing. But what I really don't understand is why Nancy decided to disclose all of this to us since nothing says "bad mother" better than letting your child tumble in a freefall to the ground. But it gives me an opening.

"I can top that," I say. This is the first time I've told this to anyone. Even Thad. "Last Friday, when it was time for Blair to take a nap, I put her in the portable swing, the one that's barely a few inches off the ground, in her room, and I strapped her in and shut the door. And she was crying, like she always does. And I let her cry, like I always do, because usually she falls asleep in ten minutes or so. And she kept crying. And crying. And about twenty minutes went by. So I peeked in her room. And the swing was swinging. But Blair wasn't in it."

The mommies gasp.

"What do you mean, she wasn't in it?" Jenn asks.

"She wasn't *in* it! She somehow slipped out of the strap and flipped over the back of the swing and was lying flat on her face on the floor *underneath* it."

"Underneath it?"

"Underneath it! I almost died. I felt like I was this monster mother who should be arrested or something."

"Oh my God, I know," Nancy says, nodding.

I stare at Nancy. She looks at me funny. I can't imagine what they would think if I told them the whole story—that I left Blair crying in her swing so long because I was checking my work e-mail and getting really annoyed that I couldn't have just ten minutes to myself to check my damn e-mail, though no one at work was expecting me to be checking my e-mail. Because it was Friday. My day off. I was not getting paid to work, not getting paid to check my e-mail. Except that I had to. I'd been aching to. I'd been watching the clock, counting down the minutes until it was a reasonable time to put Blair down to sleep so I could log on and respond to a random e-mail from my boss or from anyone, really, to prove how dedicated I was. To prove that, even though I was a mom now, and even though I was home supposedly doing mom things, they could still count on me 150 percent. And, also, to prove to myself that I still had important things to do besides plan my six-month-old's first birthday party, which is what Meridith has been stressing about this morning at Baby and Me. Actually, she's been stressing about her mother-in-law, who's started asking questions about Lucas's first birthday. A fire hall? A VFW? Gymboree? Chuck E. Cheese? But still. Does a baby's first birthday require six months of planning? Does it require a fire hall?

Maybe it does. Maybe that's the problem—I'm supposed to be paying attention to these things, to party planning and Hyland teething tablets and the benefits of organic pureed sweet peas over Gerber's pureed sweet peas. I'm supposed to be dangling toys above Blair's head every chance I get, and pulling colorful scarves out from the center of empty paper towel tubes in front of her face, and balancing her on my feet while I lie on my back, holding her hands, making zoom-zoom airplane sounds. Whenever I see the mommies, one of them pulls out a fun new vibrating toy or a light-up gadget that they've just bought to help Cailyn or Bella or Genni or Sydney learn to "reach" or learn "self-efficacy" or learn something that Blair clearly isn't learning because we're lucky if I've remembered to restock the wipes in the diaper bag, much less hand her a spoon.

How do they just know this stuff? How does this all come so naturally to them while I'm constantly following, playing catch-up, running to Babies "R" Us to buy a pack of plastic placemats that stick to tables to protect kids from germs, which every single one of the mommies pulled out of her bag when we went to Don Pablo's two Fridays ago while Blair managed to pick off a hardened blob of gum, chewed and discarded under the lip of table by someone who probably had Ebola. Meridith and her husband have already read Lucas the entire Harry Potter series. They've just started *The Chronicles of Narnia*. The most I've done is watch Blair kick her legs and flail her arms while I hold her and sing "Clang, clang, clang went the trolley." I'm supposed to be doing more than that.

I'm supposed to be mom-ing, entertaining, teaching, even though *she* isn't doing anything. *She* doesn't seem to care what I do. *She* lies on the floor or on a blanket or on her gym mat, occasionally looking up at the toys hanging from the bars that arch over her head, sometimes on her stomach, sometimes on her back, sometimes lifting her head up, sometimes not lifting it up, sometimes squealing, sometimes not squealing, sometimes smiling, sometimes not. One morning last weekend, when Thad walked into Blair's room to get her up and found her there, babbling to herself, grabbing her feet with her hands, we were so thrilled finally to have something to videotape her *doing* that we spent the entire day catching her in varying stages of feet grabbing, which in the end became a thirty-three-minute documentary of "Baby Playing with Feet."

Of course, playing with their feet is exactly what six-month-old babies are supposed to be doing. That's what the pediatrician says. That's what all the books say. I guess I just expected more at this point. I expected us to be chatting. I expected her to be reading and walking and arguing with me over the socks I picked out for her to wear. I kind of expected her to be that way right after we checked out of the maternity ward, like she'd spend her first ride in her car seat asking me questions about the ABCs. And rhododendrons. And Hemingway. Now I know better. Now I know that, when I pop in a twenty-minute Baby Einstein video, she'll be captivated for about seven minutes and then start looking at the ceiling, while I stay focused until the very end because I am now a person who can be entirely mesmerized by watching a metronome with a green plastic octopus stuck to it tick back and forth.

At least I talk to her and smile at her and laugh at her, and call her "cutie" and "buddy" and "pootron-arama." Or at least I do that on video. And she smiles back. She watches me like I'm the coolest thing since rice cereal. At least on video. But it's just so much work. I have to think about it. I have to consciously remind myself to talk to her, not to make calls on my cell phone when we're in the car and, instead, to narrate what we're doing, where we're going, and what we're passing on the street, as if reminding myself that she is, in fact, there. And that it is, in fact, my job to take care of her, to introduce her to the world. And that I, in fact, asked for this—Fridays off. To be with her.

Maybe that's the problem. Maybe she'd be better off at Jane's on Fridays. Jane seems to know what to do. Jane seems to enjoy her. And I'd be better off at work on Fridays where I know what to do, instead of home with her, dying for her to fall asleep, letting her cry in her swing for five minutes, ten minutes, twenty minutes, while I checked e-mail that I didn't need to check and then found her on the floor, under the portable swing, on her stomach where she typically hates to be, still crying. And I ran in. And I picked her up. And I held her tightly to my chest.

"I'm sorry. I'm so sorry," I said, rocking her side to side, wondering if I should call the doctor, if I should go to the emergency room, if I should give her away to someone who won't let her fall out of swings. "I'm so sorry, little one," I said, and felt tears running fast down my cheeks, so many tears that everything I looked at was blurry. I laid her down on the changing table and gently, carefully, inched my hands down her tiny arms, down her tiny legs, squeezing ever so slightly, watching for her to flinch, feeling for tiny, broken bones.

But I don't tell that part to the mommies as we're sitting on the floor at Baby and Me. I would have told them about how bad I felt, about how I cried as I picked Blair up from the floor—that's exactly the kind of thing I want people to know. That there is, in fact, a good mom inside me. Even though, in order to prove there's a good mom there, I have to first admit to being a really bad mom, to not only letting my baby cry so I can check e-mail but being pissed that she's crying and keeping me from what *I* want to do. But I don't tell them because I'm too distracted. By Nancy.

Because when I just said I felt like a monster mother for letting Blair fall out of her swing, Nancy nodded. She nodded like she gets it. Like she gets me. Maybe she feels it, too—the realization, deep in the back of her throat, that something just isn't right, that this mothering thing is harder than she ever expected it to be, that she's not exactly good at it. Staring at Nancy, surely making her so uncomfortable that she'll never speak another word to me ever again, I wonder if, maybe, I'm not so isolated and alone and horrible after all. That I really don't need to keep pretending that everything is fine. Or maybe Nancy was just being polite. But then she'd be trying to make me feel better: *Don't be so hard on yourself. You're not a terrible mother.*

Nancy didn't say that. Nancy said she knows.

• • •

I push the stroller into Baby and Me the following rainy Friday expecting a different vibe. I imagine that, after what Nancy and I confessed last week, I won't find them debating oatmeal versus mixed-grain cereal or whether the lavender calming bath soap dries out skin. And then I would know for sure that last week wasn't a fluke, that I really, truly wasn't the only one feeling like I wasn't so hot at this mommy thing. And I'd know that the relationships I'd been working so hard to develop with these women had more depth than the random advice we shared about the benefits of buying larger diapers to better contain the rainbow of poop that has presented itself since we all started introducing jarred food.

"Bella hates green beans," Nancy says as I sit down, balancing Blair in my left arm as I tug up the band of my maternity jeans.

"Lucas hates green beans, too!" Meridith shouts. "He *hates* them. I don't blame him, though. Have you tasted them?"

"They don't even taste like food," Nancy says.

167

"We tried carrots last night," I join in, not sure what makes me more of an ass: the fact that I expected my relationship with these women to be different this week or the fact that I just referred to something Blair did by using the word "we." When did I become *that* mom? How did I bypass every single other maternal instinct except *that* one? *We* tried carrots. *We* cried it out. *We* peed down the front of mommy's silk skirt.

"Cailyn *loves* carrots," Jenn says.

"Carrot poop's the worst," Nancy adds.

"I *know*," says Jenn. "And it still kind of smells like carrots."

"I think it smells more like carrots coming out than going in," I say, because what else can I say? We're talking about poop again. That, apparently, is what moms do. They talk about poop. Thad and I talk about poop, too. All the time. Ever since Blair's second day home from the hospital when Thad called to me from the changing table with such urgency that I assumed Blair's arm had fallen off.

"Vicki, come HERE!" he yelled. I sprinted in, halting in the doorway by Thad's outstretched arm. He was clutching a diaper in his hand as if it were a petrified rodent. There, in the liner, I saw the most disturbing thing I had ever seen—a clump of thick, gummy, black tar.

"Vicki, this just came out of the baby," Thad said, shouting, as if I were still in another room. I didn't speak. The diaper was barely 3 inches from my face, and I felt slightly afraid that if I moved too quickly, its contents might rear up and attack.

"Vicki, what *is* this?"

"It's meconium," I said, impressed that this term for a newborn's first poop that I'd learned during the Baby Basics class we took two and a half months ago not only remained in my brain, but was waiting in a lobe immediately accessible to a woman who had not slept in 132 hours.

"How do we get it off?" Thad asked.

"Off of where?" I asked back, looking down at the diaper, the *disposable* diaper, suddenly concerned that all my husband's previous claims of knowing how to change diapers were about as reliable as his claims of knowing how to rethread the pull rope in the lawnmower.

"Off of *her*," he said, gesturing down at the baby, whom I'd forgotten was even here, her miniature bottom entirely smeared with the poop-paste from hell. "I think we need something a little stronger than a wipe."

"Want me to get a washcloth?"

"I was thinking sandpaper," he said. I waited for him to laugh. He didn't laugh.

Neither of us realized it at the time, after soiling somewhere between eight and thirty-seven wipes, while Thad held up Blair's spindly legs and I carefully chipped at the remaining dregs of the quick-hardening butt lava with my fingernail, that this was merely the first of many conversations over the varied species of poop. A few days later, it was me calling Thad into Blair's room.

"Honey? Can you look at this? I can't tell if it's greenish yellow or yellowish green."

Then, days later: "Would you call this 'seedy'?"

Then came the nuclear rainbow, first glowing yellow, then bright green, then glowing green, pulsing almost, making me wonder if the tiny little poop curds might start dividing and growing into separate, living organisms.

And then, when Blair was just shy of four weeks old, the pooping stopped.

All the baby books I read said it was normal for nursing babies to stop pooping. But, after eight days without even a marble, I rushed her in for an emergency visit to the pediatrician. He poked up her bum with a pinky slathered in Vaseline as I leaned over her head, whispering in her ear, "It's okay, little one. It'll be over in a second," while mentally willing myself not to pass out. The doctor expected a poop geyser to shoot forth. Nothing came.

"She's fine," he assured me.

"Could this be why she's crying so much?" I asked.

"I doubt it. This is perfectly normal." And, bowelwise, she seemed fine. No straining. No swollen tummy. No trucker-like gas. We were the ones who were not fine. Already, Thad and I were drowning in things we didn't understand—breastfeeding, crying, the astounding amount of orange wax in Blair's ears. But we understood poop. We pooped, too. And when Blair pooped, even when she pooped so much that it blasted out of her diaper and up her back and into her hair, we knew something we were doing was working.

The entire family united in a Poop Watch.

"Did Blair have a BM?" My father asked when he called on the Sunday after the failed pediatric enema.

"Did Blair make stinky yet?" My grandmother asked when she called a few days later.

"Has there been any movement?" Thad's mom asked as soon as she walked in the door the following Thursday to help me take care of Blair for a few days while Thad traveled to Orlando for work.

And then, one day, just as randomly as it stopped, it started again—a diaper full of Milk Duds. I called, literally, everyone I knew. And there was much rejoicing. Thad paraded Blair around the house like she was a trophy. I took a photo. And our lives became regular again. Until now. Until the solid food. Until the call to my cell phone from Thad two nights ago while I was riding home on the rush-hour train, packed so tightly with irritated people that no one was speaking.

"Runny? What do you mean by 'runny'?" I yelled into the receiver. "Like mud? Like soup? Does it smell like carrots?"

"Did it?" Nancy asks at Baby and Me, after I finish telling this story to the mommies, just as Joan pulls up with Genni in her stroller. Joan is usually late. Joan does not usually look like she got hit by a school bus, which she does today, her dark hair half pulled back in a ponytail, her eyes slits, a smudge of what looks like sweet potatoes on her white nursing tank. "Because I've been saving the really good ones," Nancy continues. "I just fold up the diapers and leave them on the changing table so Dave can see them when he comes home."

"You do *not*," Jenn says.

"Oh, yes, I do," Nancy answers. Everyone laughs. Everyone but Joan. I feel kind of embarrassed. *Yes, we're talking about poop again. Yes, this is all we talk about. Yes, this is as real as it gets.* But I realize that Joan isn't paying attention to the conversation, which now has turned to the weird humping motion all the kids seem to be doing in bed, when they're lying on their stomachs, their butts rocking up and down. Joan is gazing at the floor, looking strangely tired, overly tired, which is odd since Genni has been sleeping through the night since she was six weeks old. She slides a water bottle out of her diaper bag. She takes a sip, twists the top back on, and puts it back. The conversation lulls.

"I think I shook Genni too hard last night," she says.

Everyone turns toward her.

"I think I shook Genni too hard," she says again, like these are the only words that will ever come out of her mouth for the rest of her life. A tear drips down her cheek, almost in slow motion.

I hear a chorus of reassuring voices—"Oh, I'm sure you didn't"; "I'm sure she's fine." I should join in. *You didn't, Joan. You just think you did, but you didn't.* It would be so easy—to placate Joan, to dilute this moment, to prevent it from getting too solemn, too real, so we can continue wading at the depth this group seems to be most comfortable in, talking about nap times and diaper brands and poop.

No one here would expect me to do anything other than join in. They don't know me or what I've been struggling with or how frustrated I've been with myself these past six months. They just know the image I'm projecting—the "good mother" with the "helpful husband" and the "challenging but completely lovable daughter," the mother who "tells funny stories about parenting" and is "happy" just like she's supposed to be in this, "the most exciting and rewarding time of her life." Plus, Genni is fine. She looks just fine. Joan probably didn't shake her at all. She's just stunned by the realization of what she could have done.

But even after the litany of reassurances, I can't help but notice how pale Joan's expression is, how naked and ashamed. Another tear runs down her face, which she catches with the back of her hand. I picture myself then, about two weeks ago when Thad was in Dallas for three days for work. And then, again, the week before, when he was in Boston overnight. Blair was crying. Blair wouldn't stop crying. And there I was, holding her, out at arm's length, gripping too tight on her chest, my head pounding with one word—*Stop*.

"I've been there, Joan," I say. I admire her. She's taking a big risk, a risk that I haven't been brave enough to take. I look her straight in the eyes as if no one else is here, as if I have to pretend we're alone to convince her that she's not. "I can't tell you how many times I've been there."

• • •

When I pick up the phone at work and hear my high school friend Krysia's voice on the other end, I know something is wrong.

"Meg asked me to call you to let you know what's going on," she says. She and Meg both live in Pittsburgh. We all went to the same high school and, before we started squatting out babies, had vacationed together in Florida every March at a home we rented on the ocean in St. Augustine, complete with hot tub and heated pool and husbands, who bonded so fraternally over the Coronas they carried around in thermal cozies decorated with photos of thonged women's asses that we wondered if, unbeknown to us, our spouses had graduated from high school together, too. We competed—like the teenagers we were when we last spent entire weeks in each other's company—over which couple could win at Cranium, and which couple could cook a more elaborate meal paired with an even more elaborate cocktail, and which couple could more elaborately decorate the table for their elaborate meal that always ended at around midnight because of so much talking and so much booze. Last year, though, things had changed a bit. Krysia called her parents every night to check on her son Eli, who had just turned one. Heidi was seven months pregnant and yet still appeared at the pool each morning wearing a more stylish bathing suit than the one she'd worn the day before. And then there was me, lounging with the other girls in lawn chairs on the second-floor porch, gazing out at the ocean that was so close we could feel tiny grains of salt in the air, sharing rather nonchalantly that I'd gone off the pill three months ago.

"You're on prenatals, right?" Krysia asked.

"On what?"

"Prenatals?"

"Pre-whats?"

"You have to start taking prenatals," she scolded, and then proceeded to explain how I needed the folic acid in prenatals to ensure that the baby I was rather nonchalantly planning to have would not have "neural tube defects," whatever "neural tube defects" were. "You should be on them too," she ordered Meg, who'd mentioned the night before that she might have started thinking about, maybe, sometime before she turns sixty, having a baby.

And she did. Three weeks ago, five months to the day after Blair was born, Meghan's husband Kevin sent out the requisite e-mail announcing the birth of 7-pound, 11-ounce, 22-inch-long Maeve to "two delighted parents," accompanied by photos of baby Maeve and her very wrinkled hands, all wrapped and hatted in the hospital with her delighted parents who did, in fact, look delighted.

I'd called Meg last week, leaving a congratulatory message, telling her I'd totally understand if she was just too tired or busy to call back, fully expecting her to call back anyway. Days passed. A week. No one called back. Then Krysia called.

Apparently, two weeks after Maeve arrived, Meg's mother had gone into the hospital to have a lump in her neck removed. The lump, it turned out, was cancerous. And worse, when the doctor was performing the surgery, there was a complication that he resolved by giving her an emergency tracheotomy, which he suspected might have to be permanent. No one knew if she would be able to speak normally ever again.

"Ever again?" I yelp to Krysia.

"Ever again," she says, again. "Meg's been in Erie with her mom for the past week. Without Maeve."

"*Without* Maeve?" I shout, certain that every intern in the corral of cubicles outside my office is now straining to hear what I'm shouting about.

"Without Maeve."

"I don't understand," I say. I don't. At all. I can't understand—I can't begin to grasp even slightly—how Meg could have gotten in a car and driven two hours away from her seven-day-old baby. And then stayed away from her. For a week.

Krysia can't understand either. Immediately, we diagnose Meg with postpartum depression. I decide it is my responsibility to intervene. As soon as I hang up the phone with Krysia, I dash off a very pointed e-mail to Meg's husband: "I want to encourage you to get Meg to her OBGYN or whomever to address the possibility of postpartum. . . . "

And he writes back: "Meg was depressed, no doubt about it. And it was difficult for her and me to determine if it was postpartum . . . but she's no longer showing any signs of depression and, in fact, is very attentive and bonded with Maeve."

Yeah, right, I think. *I'm sure their week apart has been very "bonding."*

Later that night, at home, as Thad digs the remnants of pureed green beans out of the seams in the plastic arms of the high chair while I entertain Blair, who is lying on her back on the family room carpet, sweeping my hair across her face, which makes her sigh with tickles, I tell Thad what happened to Meg.

"She might not ever speak again?" he yells, even more incredulous than I'd been earlier.

"Never again," I say. "And Meg drove to Erie to be with her mom. *Without* Maeve."

"What?"

"That's right."

"I don't understand."

"Me neither."

"Let me get this straight," Thad says, flipping the dishtowel over his shoulder and turning to face me straight on. "She might not ever speak again? *Ever?*"

I don't know how to answer Thad. He's right. What's shocking here, what's most shocking, is what happened to Meg's mom, not the fact that Meg went to Erie without her daughter. And yet I state with utter certainty that my friend has postpartum depression and that, because of the postpartum depression I've decided she has, I claim with equal certainty there's no way in hell she could possibly have bonded with her child, as if I've suddenly bought into all those proclamations from the motherhood mountaintop that I read, again and again, in the books and the magazine articles and the Websites, all pretty much decreeing that there are only two emotions for a new mom to feel: deep-dark, scary, put-your-baby-in-a-microwave postpartum depression or goo-goo, my-life-is-finally-complete, maternal bliss. As if there aren't a million, trillion feelings in the range between those two extremes. As if I hadn't experienced so many of those emotions myself just a few months ago. A few days ago. A few *hours* ago. As if I hadn't heard my friends Nancy and Joan admit in the past couple of weeks that they'd felt them too.

A couple of hours later, I sit in the glider rocker holding Blair to my breast. The light is off. The white-noise machine is humming. Blair's fuzzy hair is slightly damp from the bath Thad gave her a half hour ago, while I knelt beside him on the bathmat, watching Thad squeeze the red rubber crab toy, squirting water on her belly, listening to her cluck and gurgle. When Thad lifted her out of the tub and placed her on the yellow towel with the duck bill on the hood, she started to whimper. It was the first time I'd heard her cry all day, and she stopped like I knew she would, like she always did at the end of a bath when Thad and I belted our version of the *Gilligan's Island* theme song.

". . . with Little Blair, and Levi too, with Poppy and his Wife, with Mom and Dad, Grammy and Pappy, here on Little Blair's island."

And now, in the rocker, in the dark, it's just me. And Blair. I've been waiting for this moment since I got home from work. For the most part, I've been waiting because, as soon as she's asleep, I'm going to sprawl on the couch with Thad and watch an entire episode of *CSI*. Then Thad's going to tuck me in, like he always used to do, but on the way, we're going to tiptoe together into Blair's room and cover her with the quilt Thad's grandmother made for her when she was born. Thad's going to say, "Sweet dreams" to Blair, and then to me. And I'm going to sleep, uninterrupted, until morning.

But there's another reason why I've been waiting. At some point over the past five weeks, ever since Blair started sleeping through the night, this half hour in the rocker has become my favorite time of the day. Blair and I are both relaxed. We're both still. We're both content to be here, in the rocker, in the dark, alone, together. I can't remember the first night I felt this way. I also can't remember the first time she smiled at me, or the first time she squealed when she recognized my face through the slats in her crib when I snuck in to get her in the morning. I can't remember the change, as if I'd come to expect the bad stuff—the crying, the frustration—in the same way, at the beginning, I'd expected the bliss. I'd been expecting the wrong things all along.

But now, with her squealing, with her more at ease than she's ever been, I've forgotten. That fast. I've forgotten that just six short months ago I could not envision that I would ever be where I am right now, with a whole night of sleep ahead of me, in a bedroom without a receiving blanket or a Pack 'n Play or a single ounce of spit-up in it, in a bed with a husband I didn't want to kill. I've forgotten how scared I was, how ambivalent I was, how stressed I was. I've forgotten so entirely that when I find out my friend left her baby, I'm not understanding. I'm shocked. I assume something must be wrong with her since she clearly hadn't bonded enough with her week-old child, as if it hadn't taken me months and months to bond with mine. And I wonder if maybe that is why no one ever told me that becoming a mom was so hard. Maybe their babies had gotten older and cuter and funnier. Maybe their babies had started to smile. And squeal when they saw them. And they'd all gotten used to each other. Maybe they'd forgotten.

mommy gone wild

"[Your baby is] like a little sponge that takes in everything you do. You may not think he's aware of what's going on around him, but he is."

—*Your Baby's First Year: Week by Week*

I'm stepping off the bus in the parking lot of a hotel in Cape May on the Jersey Shore when I realize I've forgotten the funnels for the breast pump packed in the black nylon breast-pump case that I'm carrying over my shoulder so it looks like a purse.

This is not good. The funnels are only the most important part of the breast pump: they cup the breasts in an airtight seal so the breasts can, in fact, be pumped. And they need to be pumped. Because I am working. I am, again, with the staff of *Philadelphia* magazine, along with the rest of the company—the accounting department, the advertising department, the marketing department, the CFO, the president, the chairman. I've arrived at the annual company outing. A warm September weekday at the shore. Drinking margaritas. Eating lobster. A lovely reward for this morning when Blair decided the mixed-grain cereal she eats for breakfast every day had turned evil and needed to be discharged from her mouth and massaged into her hair.

The funnel problem is especially not good because I'm not wearing a bra. This is the first time I've not worn a bra since Blair was born. For the first few months, I even slept in my bra, my boobs and their excretions far too unruly to permit them free reign. And they hurt, at first from stretching to twenty-seven times their normal size, then from sucking, and recently from biting with those two white teeth buds starting to poke through Blair's bottom gum like claws. But mostly, they hurt from filling up faster than I've been deflating them. I used to be stringent—nurse Blair at 7:00, pump at work at 10:00, at 1:00, at 4:00, and nurse Blair before bed. Then I started to forget, pumping at 11:00 or noon, turning the rest of the day into a frantic pump fest, fearing that my body would stop thinking it needed to produce milk and would stop producing it. And Blair would starve.

Eventually, I rationalized that I could pump just as much if I only pumped twice, not realizing that waiting four hours between pumpings meant that my boobs would become so full, and the hydrant-like pressure inside them would thump with such pain, that I couldn't tolerate even a wrinkle in my shirt anywhere around my chest. And now, here I am, far from home, far from Blair, pumpless and braless, which makes the black summer dress with the spaghetti straps that actually fit when I tried it on this morning, that actually looked cute, that actually made me forget the new varicose vein I'd discovered a few days ago behind my right knee, seem like a square of toilet paper, completely incapable of concealing what is about to transpire beneath it.

If only I had some idea of what is about to transpire beneath it. The longest I've gone without pumping or nursing is five hours. It is 10:00 AM, three hours since I last nursed Blair. We are not supposed to leave the shore until 4:00, six hours from now. Which means my boobs will be mounting for nine hours straight. Will this dress be able to contain them? Will they start to spray? How will I ever explain the mile of paper towels I'll have to drag out of the dispenser in the bathroom and wrap, twenty or so times, around my chest? What if there are no paper towels? What if there's just an air dryer? Then what? What will the ladies in accounting think when they stroll in for a pee and see me, slamming my hand over and over again on the silver button, arching back underneath the nozzle pointed directly at my nipple that's erupting in a fountain of milk?

"Guess how stupid I am? I totally forgot to bring all the parts of my breast pump," I say to the credit manager as we're walking through the front doors of the hotel, figuring that my best defense here is a good offense, and a good offense in this particular circumstance is telling as many people as I possibly can what I've done so there's no question what's going on when I'm spotted pacing along the shoreline, holding two plastic beer cups under my chest to catch the runoff.

"Can you believe I forgot my breast pump?" I say to the marketing manager as we maneuver our chairs into the tiny triangle of shade under the one branch from the one tree overhanging the hotel's outdoor patio, balancing our plates to prevent the corn on the cob from rolling over the cornbread and into the lobster tail.

"I'm such an asshole. I left my breast pump at home," I say to the new style editor, just hired last week, as we sit on the edge of the hotel pool, our legs dangling in the water because it's somewhere around 175 degrees today, causing my scalp to sweat so profusely that three people have asked if I took a dip in the ocean. It is just after 2:00. I grow slightly concerned when, behind the protection of the gigantic sunglasses I bought last week at Target, I peer down at my chest for the 4,532nd time in the past four hours and notice that my boobs are sticking straight out. I lean back, hoping the angle forces them to stand down and fold against the top of my stomach. But, no matter how far back I lean, they hold forth, pointing at the buffet table, at the roof, at the sky, like guns on an army tank, preparing to fire.

I jump up, grab my nylon bag, and speed-walk through the doors into the lobby. I head to room 101, the one the magazine reserved for the day in case people needed a place to change or "in case you need some privacy to do your thing," explained the office manager, winking at me. I open the door. I call out.

"Hello? Anyone in here?"

No one answers. I don't trust the silence, skulking into the room, peering on each side of the two double beds covered with quilted spreads pockmarked with pastel seashells of varying sizes and shapes. I step into the bathroom, closing and locking the door behind me. I grab a white hotel towel and fold it in half, resting it on the edge of the tub as a pillow. I untie the straps on my dress, letting the top fall around my waist. I turn and wiggle the knob on the door to make sure I've definitely locked it. I kneel down, folding my body over the pillow so my boobs are now aiming at the anti-slip strips coating the floor of the tub. I grab hold with my hands. I squeeze. Nothing. I squeeze again. Nothing. I wrap both hands around my right boob and squeeze, nothing. *I am trying to milk myself*, I think. *In a tub. In a hotel room. At the shore.* I switch up the motion, rubbing my fingers down the sides. Nothing. It's as if they're too full. As if I waited too long. As if the only option at this point is for them to detonate.

On the bus ride back, I sit next to the editorial assistant. She has been drinking beer since 10:00. She is describing her wedding dress because I asked her to, intending to call attention away from all things boob-related. She is talking close, leaning in next to my ear as if the details of her wedding dress are a secret that can't be revealed to the ad assistants sitting behind us. Her shoulder nudges against my shoulder, forcing my body to slant toward the window, my right boob knocking against the armrest, actually making a sound when it hits because it is currently as hard and as big as a very unripe cantaloupe.

"Oh my GOD!" I yell, pain shooting up my chest into the back of my neck. I twist my arms around each other, holding them in front of my chest as if the position will somehow redirect the pain pathways in my body.

"What happened?" the assistant says, placing her hand on my shoulder. I flinch.

"My boobs," I say, huffing, realizing I hadn't breathed since the initial collision. "They're rocks."

"Because you forgot your pump?"

"Exactly."

"Holy shit," she says. Then she reaches out, her arm stretching over the protective cage of my own. She extends her pointer finger. And, before I know it, she pokes. On the top. Of my left boob.

•　　　•　　　•

When I walk into the studio the next morning for the first of the Music Together classes the mommies and I have signed up for, I can't speak. The woman who teaches the class—Miss Jeannie—is far too cute. And thin. And young. And she sings. Constantly. From the moment the class starts until it ends, she sings. And she sings well. And I kind of want to push her over. Just knock her down, like this hyperactive two-year-old named Jack is doing to all our seven-month-olds. He needs a leash, I think. And I need a mask or something to hide my face. I see the other moms watching me. I see them cracking up, particularly when Miss Jeannie pulls out a big bag of maracas and two stacks of straw sombreros, a stack of little ones for kids and a stack of big ones for moms, and begins to lead us in a circle around the mat while singing a Spanish song. Everyone but me seems to know the words. Probably because the lyrics are in the Good Mother Manual, complete with sheet music, that the nurse on the maternity ward clearly decided not to give me after I asked, for the third time, for an extra pair of those fabulous hospital-issue mesh underwear I still secretly wear once or twice a week.

"Palo, palo, palo, palo, palito, palo ay," everyone sings. I mouth the wrong words, a beat or two behind everyone else, thinking to myself, *Is this real?*

What *is* real is that my boobs are throbbing. After the fiasco at the shore yesterday, after feeling tickles streaming down my stomach while waiting an hour in rush-hour traffic during the drive from the bus back home, looking down and discovering that the entire front of my black cotton dress was soaking wet with breast milk, I decided that this might be a good time to wean Blair from breast milk during the day. I'd still nurse her at night and in the morning, just like the other mommies were doing, except they'd cut the daytime feedings long ago, when they went back to work, because they knew pumping would be a hassle, because they are all much smarter than I am. I've already survived the worst of the weaning process—the first day. Amy said that, during the first week, it hurt to breathe. But, eventually, her boobs stopped filling up. Mine, however, are still filling. In fact, they're almost filled, right now, in music class, which is why I'm dodging the silk scarves the older kids are waving, afraid a scarf might flutter by my chest, might touch my chest, which might be just enough pressure to inspire me to scream out and send all these children into therapy for the rest of their lives.

Miss Jeannie hands out instruments for the kids to play during the Bongo Jam. I grab a pair of red sticks for Blair and hand them to her. She's propped in my lap, facing the center of the room. She can't quite sit up without weeble-wobbling over. And I can see over her shoulder that she has placed the sticks in her mouth. Other moms are frantically pulling the dirty sticks out of their babies' mouths. I am not. I'm just so relieved that she isn't leaning against my aching chest, and even more relieved that she isn't crying, I'll pretty much let her do anything at all. Then Lucas's mom, Meridith, points over at us. She says something, but I can't hear her over the music. She points again. "Look at Blair," I hear her say. And I look down.

Blair is banging the sticks together like she is the first person on earth who ever thought to do so. She's smiling in a way I've never seen her smile before, huge and wide. She's huffing and puffing, her breath pulsing in the first indication of an actual laugh. And her eyes. Her eyes are all bright and crisp and attentive. And she's banging. Banging away. I start to laugh. Really loud, as if Blair and I are the only two people in the room. She looks at me, and bangs and smiles, and bangs and smiles. And I think that she's figured it out. That I'm the mommy. That I'm the one person in this world who might care about her banging two red sticks together. And I do care, which is equally surprising to me. And she can tell. *Look, Mommy. I'm banging sticks. I'm. Banging. Sticks!*

● ● ●

A few weeks later, I meet some of the mommies at a bar on Route 73 for a girls' night out. We look completely un-mommy-like sitting on the outdoor patio, hair blown out, lipstick on, sipping red wine, not a single nugget of spit-up on us anywhere. Jenn pulls out a pack of Marlboro Lights she bought at Wawa for the occasion, and as I take the first hit off the first cigarette I've smoked in more than a year, I wonder if we would ever have become friends if we'd met before there were babies. Meridith? She's practically a baby herself. Joan is ten years older than I am. Amy gets up at 6:00 AM to work out. Nancy's wedding dress was an exact replica of the one Kate Winslet wore in *Titanic*, and she keeps it hanging in a glass case in the corner of her bedroom. Would the women we used to be have had anything to talk about? Would we have even liked each other?

Of course, the woman I used to be didn't need these women to be my friends. I had plenty of friends. But those friends didn't seem to have much in common with me anymore, leaving me in a bizarre friendship limbo. As much as I'd tried to pretend that everything was the same, that I was the same, as much as I'd resisted putting up photos of Blair in my office as if the lack of evidence would make my friends at work forget I was a "mom," I wasn't getting away with it. I *was* a "mom" now, a "mom" who could no longer spontaneously go out for a drink after work, who couldn't meet at the Happy Rooster on Thursday nights to sing karaoke until the bar closed, who barely had enough energy to read the instructions on the bottle of infant Tylenol, much less the profile in the *New Yorker* that everyone was raving about over Pad Thai at the lunch table in the office last week. When I called to catch up with friends from college who didn't have kids, I didn't know what to say when they asked what was going on with me, embarrassed that all I could think to tell them was that Blair found her voice, and Blair took her first shower with her daddy, and Blair went to her first birthday party last Sunday in a darling pink-and-orange, madras-plaid dress. I was now a woman who drove a minivan. I was now a woman who carried Wet Ones in her purse. I was now a woman who thought that the most subversive thing she could do on a Friday night was go to a bar with a bunch of new moms and smoke a cigarette.

"Dave would kill me if he knew I was smoking," Nancy says, blowing the smoke up over her shoulder to keep it off her clothes. "He's totally freaked out. He wanted to know exactly when I was going to leave and exactly when I was going to get home. I left him a list—'Give her bottle,' 'Put her in crib,' 'Shut off light.'"

"Thad's freaked, too," I say. I don't know why I say it. Thad's not nervous at all, even though tonight will be the longest he's ever been alone with Blair.

"Yeah, but . . ." Nancy says, then stops short. She takes a swig from her rum and Diet Coke. "I had to have sex with Dave every day this week in order to come out tonight."

"WHAT?" someone yells.

"You're kidding, right?" Paula says, her eyes bulging out of her head so far that it looks like it hurts.

"Nope."

"Every day?"

"Every. Single. Day." Nancy giggles, as if hoping this tidbit might elicit the same reaction that her pa-pasan story did at Baby and Me. It doesn't. No one laughs. Not really. We all just look at each other, and at Nancy. I figure everyone's thinking, *What a dick*. That's not what I'm thinking. I'm thinking, *Thank God I'm not the only one who thinks her own husband is a pain in the ass*. Not that Thad has been a pain in the ass lately. Tonight he wasn't a pain in the ass. Tonight he practically shoved me out the door.

"We'll be fine," he assured me. "Just go. Do something for yourself. Go!"

And he wasn't a pain in the ass when he took the monitor to the guest bedroom when we were crying it out, or when he assumed all responsibility for giving Blair her baths, or when he held and bounced and shushed her as she cried for the entire two hours we spent at a picnic at Jenn and Ryan's house in July, shrugging his shoulders as if to say, "I guess that's what love is" when Nancy's husband, Dave, commented, "I've never seen a baby cry so much. I don't know how you two do it."

But it still didn't feel to me like the two of us *were* doing it. Thad had been traveling for work every other week—even though he swore back in February that this new job would require less travel than his old one—which meant I had to leave my office almost two hours early and run to catch the train, pick Blair up, feed her, put her to bed, and then get her up in the morning to do "my" job of getting her dressed and fed and to day care by 8:00. Plus, I had to pick up the slack for everything else. So, even when he wasn't traveling, I was still writing out the bills. And getting estimates for new carpet in the hallway. And making sure we hung the meter reading on the front door on days when the gas man was coming. And remembering that the gas man was coming. And taking off work when the guy came to reseal the driveway, and when

Blair had her six-month checkup, and when Jane called on a Tuesday morning to cancel day care because she had the flu. I felt like I was supposed to be a full-time everything, and he was supposed to be just part-time.

I hear a cackle behind me and look over at the bar. There's a woman standing there, late forties or early fifties, wearing so much makeup I can see her burgundy lip liner from 15 feet away. She's standing with two friends, all the same age, all in such low-cut, scooping blouses that when the short one turns to flip her hair, I swear her nipple might pop out and say hello. The cackler cackles again, leaning in closer to the gray-haired man sitting on the stool next to her, wearing those soft Italian leather loafers that scream, at the same time, "divorced" and "mob." The cackler is talking too loudly, nervously loud, the same way I used to in high school when we snuck into fraternity parties downtown, at the TKE house across the street from my church, acting like I was someone I wasn't, older, cooler, confident. *That's going to be me*, I think. Ten years from now, I'll be divorced, doing it all over again, at a bar, in heels that make my hips ache, sipping a chocolate martini because I'll think it's still in vogue, a babysitter at home with Blair, who I'll pretend doesn't exist as I flirt, too loudly, with a chubby man in leather slippers. *That's going to be me. That's going to be Nancy and me.*

"So Ryan tells me today that he wants to have friends over tonight," Jenn spits out, as if she's been holding her breath with this information since she sat down. "Um. Hello? I told him weeks ago that we were going out. *One* night. That's all. And he invites friends over. And I'm like, 'Well, *I* won't be there.'"

No. It won't be Nancy and me trying to pick up men at a bar. It will be Jenn and Nancy and me. I giggle under my breath. I'm so wound up by the conversation that's unfolding here at this table that I sit on my hands to contain myself, not wanting to jinx what I am sure is the first real, honest-to-God, collectively intimate moment this group has ever shared, like I'm trying to prevent myself from saying something stupid like, "You have no idea how happy I am that your husband's an ass," or, "I thought I was the only one!" or "I love you guys!" Instead, I tell them something I haven't been able to say out loud since it happened, primarily because I didn't have anyone to tell. None of my friends would have understood.

"I was so mad at Thad a few months ago that I packed all of Blair's stuff into a bag . . . like, all of it. As soon as he walked in the door, I said, 'I'm going to my parents' house.'"

"You did *not*," Joan says.

"I did," I say, feeling like I'd just dropped 50 pounds out of my head and onto the wooden deck below us. I laugh. And then Jenn laughs. And Nancy.

And Joan and Paula and Michelle. We're all laughing. Everyone. Laughing. I wonder if they're thinking what I'm thinking—that we are all, to one degree or another, full of shit. Marriage-with-children? It isn't all loving and la-la like we've all been pretending it is. Our husbands? They're not all helpful and proactive and patient, like we've been pretending they are. Being a new mom—actually having this little person who depends on you to know how to be a mother and to do it right? It's not as instinctual and easy and fun as we've been acting like it is. It's not just me. It's not just Joan. It's not just Nancy. And yet here we are, seven months into motherhood, unable to tell the truth of how we feel until we escape—no babies, no husbands, a tiny bit drunk—and are finally willing to take a chance.

"I told my husband, 'The baby and I, we are a team,'" Jenn says. "'You? You do not have to be part of this team. If I go, she goes.'"

"Exactly," I say, surprised at how definitive I am when I say this, how natural it feels to agree with her—not about leaving, but about the baby, about my relationship with the baby. *The baby and I, we are a team.*

We're all still chuckling, but now we're sitting back in our chairs as if we're trying to digest it all. There's more to say. But it feels like it might be too much. At least for now, tonight, since we all just discovered that, really, we don't know each other at all. I look over at Nancy. She's sitting beside me, her hands wrapped around her drink, her fingernails tapping on the glass. She's looking straight ahead, expressionless, as if she's daydreaming. Then she leans over just a little, so her mouth is close to my left ear.

"Do you really fight with Thad?" she whispers.

"We fight."

"I mean, do you *really* fight?" She looks into her lap.

"Yeah," I say. "We *really* fight."

•　　•　　•

When Blair and I come home from music class next Friday, I open all the windows in the house.

"We need to air out this place," I say to Blair, and she looks back at me like she completely understands what I said and, in fact, agrees. It's warm for the first week in October, in the 70s, far too warm for the red stretch pants and light blue cardigan that I dressed Blair in this morning. I leave her on the floor in the family room with the rainbow stacking rings in front of her, as I run from room to room lifting the panes. Blair is sitting up, because this past weekend she started sitting up on her own, all of a sudden, as if she'd known how to do it for months but just didn't feel like it, her back ramrod straight in perfect posture like her father's. I am on the last window, on the completely opposite side of the house, in my bedroom, when I hear the crying.

She's tired. I know she's tired. I know it's nap time. But I still run like something's wrong, like my legs have their own sensors in them, completely independent of my brain, down the hall, through the living room, into the kitchen where I can now see her, toppled over on her right side, hugging the cordless phone, her head slightly propped up on the *Goodnight Moon* board book I attempted to read her this morning, though all she wanted to do was gnaw on the back cover. I carry Blair to her crib. I turn on the noise machine. I jimmy down the Venetian blind in the middle window, twisting the blinds in the opposite direction to see if they might be darker that way.

"It's not dark enough in here," I say to Blair, who is still crying, though slightly less so now that she's cuddled up with the lavender velvet blanket edged with satin that my mother thinks she's starting to become attached to, which is why I ran out to Babies "R" Us last weekend and bought two more.

The doorbell rings as I'm pulling her door closed behind me. Levi's bark echoes from back in my bedroom, his footsteps galloping down the hall, barely making the turn into the dining room as he charges toward the door to the porch that I close in the nick of time.

"No!" I yell through the door as Levi leaps 4 feet into the air so he can see through the window. I turn, then, to see for myself who is standing outside. My heart jumps. It jumps all the way into my throat and then falls into my stomach, just as fast, as if it might project right down my leg and onto the floor I retiled last spring.

"Did someone dial 911?" The policeman asks through the screen.

"No," I say. I giggle. He does not giggle.

"Someone in this house dialed 911 a few minutes ago," he says, smiling like he knows something I don't know. *It finally happened*, I think. One of the neighbors finally called the cops on me, finally realized she couldn't listen to this crying baby anymore without doing something, without helping that poor child. *Why did I open the windows?* I listen with my bionic ears, which is what Thad calls them since, over the past seven months, my hearing has evolved to such precision that I'm frequently able to hear Blair crying before she even starts crying. And, right now, there's no crying. Blair is already asleep.

"It's just me and my daughter here, and she's seven months old. We just got home," I say, wishing Levi would shut up. Or die.

"Okay," the cop says, the word more of a question than a statement, as he peers over my shoulder at Cujo, then past Cujo, as if expecting to see a conga line of thieves in black ski masks, frozen, mid-toss, with the white lacquered glider rocker suspended halfway out of the dining room window.

"Okay," I say. "Sorry for the confusion." I turn and crack open the door from the porch to the house, sliding through while Levi attempts to burrow his nose directly through my right femur. As I walk toward the kitchen, I scan through the Rolodex in my brain of every interaction I've ever had with every one of my neighbors, checking off the suspects one by one— she's not home during the day; she made us a coffee cake when we moved in. As soon as I walk past the stove and have a clear view into the family room, I remember. Blair had toppled over on *Goodnight Moon.* Blair had been crying. Blair had been clutching the cordless phone.

Blair called 911.

I lean down and pick up the phone off the floor. I dial Thad's office number.

"You are not going to believe what Blair just did . . ." I say, opening with the same phrase he's heard practically every time I've called him at work during the past seven months. Except this is the first time I'm laughing.

hope springs maternal

"You are doing the most important job in the world."

—*The Baby Book*

I wake, startled, my heart thumping as if I'd accidentally tumbled out of bed onto the floor. I squint at the clock: 1:24. Thad left for Boston yesterday to teach a training class. He'll be gone for three days. And three nights.

I'm fuzzily nodding off when I hear it again. The sound. The sound I swore woke me up and then convinced myself was just in my dream. *It's just the heat clicking on*, I think, knowing full well that the heat would not have to start up again so soon. *Calm down.* My heart is strumming too fast now to calm down. Then I think I hear it again.

Before Blair was born, when Thad traveled out of town, I'd always go through one night just like this one, hearing things, imagining, panicking, and I'd always do two things to put my mind at ease: First, I'd lock the door to the basement, assuming that barrier would deter an intruder who'd been staking our house for weeks, well aware that our pathetic, seventy-five-year-old basement windows could be opened with a pair of toenail clippers. Or, at least, I'd hear him break down the door to the basement and would have enough time to escape though the door from the bedroom to the back deck. Second, I'd lock the door to my bedroom, my first instinct as I'm lying here now, my eyes finally adjusting to the dark, wondering if Thad's aluminum baseball bat is still leaning in the corner, where I put it two weeks ago when he flew to Los Angeles for two days. But I can't lock my door. Because Blair is on the other side of my door. Blair is down the hallway, 50 feet away from me. But she is behind the first door the intruder will come across when he begins his hunt through the house.

I should shut off the baby monitor. That way, when he thunders into my room, skipping Blair's because he's been watching, because he knows that my window was the last to have a light shining through the blinds, he might not realize that there is even a child in the house, even if she wakes up, even if she starts crying. Unless he doesn't skip her room. Unless he creeps in there and, instead, I hear the sounds though the monitor on the nightstand. *The sounds of what? What would he do to her?*

I throw the covers off, realizing that I'm sweating, my breath fast and uneven as I open my bedroom door and tiptoe down the hall. My hands tremble. I open Blair's door, careful to keep my body sideways, to not turn my back entirely from the doorway to the dining room. I can hear her breathing. I back out, turn, and walk through the dining room, through the living room to the front door. Locked. Back through the living room, the dining room, into the kitchen, into the family room, to the sliding glass door. Locked. *There is no one here, Vicki. Go back to sleep*, I think.

Then, I peer down the stairs to the basement. It's black. I reach out to grab the doorknob, intending to pull it closed, to twist the key. *You have to go down. You have to. It's all up to you.* Without turning my head, I slide my left hand along the wall until I feel the light switch. I flick it on. A second passes. Nothing happens. *He cut the electric*, I think, just as the fluorescent light at the bottom of the steps starts to flicker. I march down the stairs, pretending that I'm just going down to check on the laundry, turning on the light in the laundry room. Nothing. Turning on the light on the carpeted side, jogging around the kitchen table we have no room for upstairs, over to the corner with the pull-out couch and Xbox that Thad calls the Man Room, opening the door to the workshop. Nothing.

I walk back to the bedroom, feeling silly, shutting off lights in my wake. I stop again at Blair's room, open the door, cross to the crib. She's lying on her stomach, her head turned to the right, her little thumb in her mouth. I pull the purple blanket over her back, tuck it around the sides of her body. I stare at her for a full minute, leaning along the side of the crib as if the adrenaline coursing through my veins for the past fifteen minutes has evaporated through my skin, leaving me limp and exhausted. I feel my eyes start to well, before the thought that's motivating them completely surfaces in my brain. And then, there it is. I am imagining what I would be thinking if there really were an intruder. I hear what would be running through my mind in the midst of it all.

I have to see Blair. I have to get to Blair.

●   ●   ●

We walked to the beach from the cruise ship docked in St. George, Bermuda, practically hiking for the last quarter-mile on a dirt road. This is a work trip, one part of a travel section the magazine is publishing next March on family vacations. My article is called

"Travel with Baby." For us, "Travel with Baby" in-cludes a footnote titled "Travel with Poppy and Nana," the names we finally settled on last month for my father and mother, who are staying in a cabin two doors down from us. After four days on board, I'm not sure how "Travel with Baby" would be possible with-out "Travel with Poppy and Nana," or at least without "Travel with a Second Room Occupied by People You Know So You Can Hang Out in There with the Baby Monitor and Thus Not Have to Sit in the Dark Read-ing with a Flashlight Every Night after 8:00, When the Baby Goes to Sleep in Her Pack 'n Play That Takes Up One-Third of Your Cabin."

I need this vacation. I've been telling people daily at work: "I need this vacation." Most of the people at work smirk when I say this. Of course, most of them don't have children and presume that I just *returned* from a vacation, a nearly-four-month vacation, during which they pictured me lounging on the couch watching Netflix movies while my newborn gently slept. I need this vacation, especially, because Blair has started waking up again at night, once or twice, cry-ing, accompanied by a constantly stuffy nose that she twirls away whenever I try to wipe it with a tissue, leaving a perpetual trail of shiny snot across her cheek. The runny nose, the mommies say, is a symptom of teething, as is the waking up at night, as are the two tall, fully-formed baby teeth sticking up from the center of Blair's bottom gum. Nancy has been rubbing Bella's gums with Anbesol practically since she was born as a preventive measure, though Bella is still screaming all day long with the pain of it. Blair, uncharacteristically, is not. Blair, I assume, can tolerate anything after suffering so much in her first five months, when she was starving to death on my feeble boobs—my latest diagnosis for why she was so miserable for so long since the doctor never pronounced on the colic and, now that it seems to be over, now that her legs and arms have caught up and are as chubby and squeezable as her cheeks, there is no point in discussing it anymore. She's been holding her head up, her neck steady, since she was four weeks old, while most kids continued bobbleheading for months, as if she needed to exert some kind of power, some kind of control over the shitty situation that was her life.

But, even so, Blair is waking up at night again. And crying. I try to let her cry it out. I should. But it's harder now than it was three months ago. Now she knows who I am. She smiles when I walk into a room. Sometimes she wiggles. And it makes me feel like a rock star. Or Jesus. Or the mother of Jesus. So listening to her cry, especially when I *know* that she could be hurting, is no longer endurable. In fact, it's now painful to me, because I lie there, imagining what could be hurting, imagining more pain than could ever realistically be hurting Blair but imagining it so completely that my gums start to ache. And I go in. I nurse her, even though my body only produces milk in the morning and at bedtime anymore since I stopped pumping last month, and even then barely any at all. Because it calms me. But, it's also started to calm her. Being near me. Being close to *me*. *I* calm her. It feels good to know that, finally, I can calm her.

It probably also feels good to the people who are sleeping in the cabins on either side of us that I can calm the baby next door who's screaming in the middle of the night. I only needed to do that a few times, on the first two nights, when Blair seemed confused over where she was and why there were beach towels draped over the top of her Pack 'n Play to make it as dark in there as it is in her room at home.

Or maybe all the constant attention is wearing her out, all the "wook at dose big boo eyes" and "I can hardly remember my kids at that age," accompanied by serial toe-grabbing by the grandparents cruising with us, who make up about 90 percent of the people on this ship, including a large majority in wheelchairs towing oxygen, always cornering us while we are perpetually in line for the perpetual buffet. Though nothing compares to the staff who swarm our table at dinner in the Seven Seas restaurant, the busboys and water-fillers and dessert cart pushers who barely speak a word of English, most of them from South American countries stamped in black on their nametags, fluttering white linen napkins in front of Blair's face, playing peek-a-boo with her from behind the banquet. I don't understand all the attention until the hostess from Paraguay stops by with a soupspoon to replace the one Blair hurled across the room.

"All my workers miss their babies. We are on ship for six months," she says, smiling at Blair, who is smiling back, showing off her two cartoon teeth, giggling as if we had a talk while we were on the elevator up to the Marina Deck, as if I knew and told her to be especially nice to all the people in polyester tuxedo vests. The waitress sitting with her now—so shy a moment ago she couldn't look me in the eye as she nodded again and again at Blair and then at the seat next to Blair, until I nodded back in the universal signal of "Yes, you can sit next to my baby"—is leaning into Blair, her arm wrapped around Blair's shoulders, quietly humming as she nuzzles her nose in the soft fuzz on the back of Blair's head.

"Do you want to hold her?" I ask, but before I even finish the sentence, the hostess interrupts.

"Oh . . . no, no, no. We are not allowed to hold the babies," she says. She observes the scene for a second, then tilts her head toward the woman snuggling close to Blair. "She hasn't seen her baby girl for six months. Her baby girl just turned one."

I don't process the math of this for several hours, not until I am lying in my bunk, awake, just after

1:00 AM, waiting for Blair to stir, to cry out, though I know she won't. She didn't cry when we put her down. She didn't even whine. She is tired. I am tired. But I'm waiting, nonetheless, practically rapping my fingers on the wall, like I want her to wake up, like I want her to need me, so I can crawl down the length of my bed, pull back the towel, reach over the bar, and rub her back, shushing. *Shuuuush. Mommy's here.* Those words play over and over in my head. *Mommy's here.* Even though I've been there, even though I stayed home with her for four months and have kissed her little forehead at least once every day since she was born, I'm not sure I was any more present, or attentive, or available than that woman tonight at dinner, a mother who hadn't even seen her child since she was five months old, who was holding Blair against her chest so tightly I wondered if she might never let go. Those mothers didn't even get to see all the firsts, all the milestones, all the tongues sticking out and the smiles and the rolling around on the floor. I did see all that. And, yet, I barely appreciated any of it.

The next day, we begin the hike down the side of the cliff toward the beach, my father pushing the stroller, Thad with his seersucker shirt unbuttoned and hanging open, my mother lagging behind to take photos, me blowing up the plastic beach ball Thad won in the putting contest yesterday on the Odyssey Deck. We've already been assured that the beach at our next stop, in Hamilton, is more like the postcards, that the sand is actually white and the beach is actually large, unlike this odd strip along the water that smells more like a lake. But, still, this is Blair's first trip to an ocean. When Thad carries her into the calm water, dipping her toes into the surf, she looks nothing but confused. Like she can't decide whether to throw up or cry. Until she does decide.

But the crying stops when we lay her down on her stomach on the navy-blue-and-white-striped beach chair, hoping the tropical air will numb her to sleep. She doesn't sleep. Instead, she reaches out, over the edge of the chair, leaning down until she rests the tips of her fingers on the damp sand. She doesn't pull away, or cringe from the weird sensation of the grit, but instead starts to dig, instinctually, the way a dog starts paddling before his feet even hit the water, until she's dug down so far she can no longer reach the bottom of her little hole. She looks up at me. Her eyes are bright, as if she's saying, "Have you *touched* this?" I reach down and scratch my nails through the sand, leaving a patch of plowed lines, feeling the individual grains, the stickiness, the itchiness like I've never felt anything before.

•   •   •

The phone rings. It's my mother. She and my dad are on the Pennsylvania Turnpike, driving back to Erie after the cruise. My mom forgot to tell me that when she went grocery shopping for us yesterday, she stopped at the Halloween store in the same plaza and saw the perfect costume for Blair.

It hadn't even occurred to me that we needed to buy a Halloween costume for Blair, much less that Halloween was even approaching, until I got an e-mail from Joan, the photographer-mom, who invited the rest of the mommies and daddies to her house so she could take a series of photos of the kids in their costumes. If there were any reason why we should buy Blair a costume, it would be to take a photo of her in the costume so there would be a photo in her baby album of "Baby's First Halloween." We certainly wouldn't be taking Blair out trick-or-treating, partly because the township only allows trick-or-treating in daylight when we're both at work and partly because she wouldn't understand why the hell we were carrying her all over the neighborhood with a bag. But mostly because I'd just signed up for Weight Watchers, clocking in at 13 pounds over my pre-pregnancy weight, and it would be Points Plan suicide for me to even think about a Mounds Bar, much less have many of them sitting in a bowl on the counter next to the coffeepot.

I drive up to the Halloween store and I find the ladybug costume my mother described, all fuzzy and warm-looking, with an adorable pair of red antennae screwed into a black headband. Blair would look very cute in this outfit, as if there were a baby on the planet who would not look cute dressed as a ladybug. But I just can't do it. I can't reach up and pull down the plastic bag. It all feels too cliché—cute kid dressed as cute insect—especially since nothing about Blair's life thus far has felt cliché. All these costumes—the flower, the pumpkin, the bulgy-eyed frog—would look so inappropriate on her, as if I were trying to prove something. *See, mommies, she IS sweet, after all!*

Just as I'm about to turn and leave, I spy another costume hanging on the rack below, tucked behind what looks like a Power Ranger suit, if only I knew what a Power Ranger was. I pull it out. I check the size. I walk directly to the register and hand the cashier enough to cover the $13.99 price tag, which seems too expensive for the other costumes, but not for this one.

The next day, I read in the free local paper that there's a parade down Haddon Avenue the night before Halloween. Blair might enjoy a parade. Kids will be marching in costumes. There will be high school bands and fire trucks and Civil War re-enactors and trick-motorcycle riders. *We* might enjoy the parade. And Blair will get to wear her costume more than once. And people will see her. And we can take pictures so we're sure not to have a gaping hole in the photo album where better parents would have a collage of Halloween stills.

It's oddly warm the night of the parade. Thad pulls a blue hoodie over his head, and I wear his fleece jacket with only a T-shirt underneath. We dress Blair and pack her into the stroller, wrapped in a white blanket with little yellow ducks all over it that kind of ruin the effect of her costume. We walk the four blocks to Haddon Avenue and stand on the corner next to a planter filled with bright red mums. Thad lifts Blair out of her stroller, into the air, and over his head, maneuvering her legs around his neck for her first-ever ride on her daddy's shoulders.

"Look at the little baby!"

"Look how cute!"

"She's so cute!"

We hear the chorus all around us as people look up and spot Blair, this baby, this infant, in a red bodysuit with black foam wings sprouting out the back and a red skull-cap with two black foam horns protruding out near her temples.

Because Blair is dressed as a devil.

•   •   •

"I just have to say, we all loooove the way you guys dress," says the public relations girl whose name, I

think, is Jessica. I'm sitting with a group of my col-
leagues in the VIP section at the Red Square restaurant at the Tropicana in Atlantic City. It is Friday
night. I've been in Atlantic City since lunch and will
not be leaving until sometime tomorrow morning because the chamber of commerce invited the magazine
staff to come for a night to make sure we were well
aware of how cool it was, how Vegas it was, how much
we should be writing about it. I'd lived in Philadelphia
for almost five years and I'd never made the hour-long
drive to Atlantic City, which probably was why, when
my boss sent out the e-mail two weeks ago to the
people on staff he wanted to come on the trip, he
typed his new favorite word: "mandatory."

I opened the e-mail first thing when I got into the
office and immediately began plotting how to get out
of the trip. First of all, Fridays are my days off. I don't
get paid to work on Fridays. I don't have day care
on Fridays. Blair has music class on Fridays. Except.
I could switch days off that week. I could ask Jane if
she could take care of Blair that Friday. I could, theo-
retically, go to Atlantic City. I e-mail Thad and outline
the situation. Thad writes back. He suggests I go to
Atlantic City, but he'll save me by calling my cell
phone when I'm there, sometime around 9:00 at night,
with a "Blair Emergency" so I'll have an excuse to
leave. "Things that qualify," he writes: "Slipper falls
off; new tooth appears; prehensile tail appears; says

'momma'; says 'dada'; says, 'what a day with Jane and the other kids' and heads for the liquor cabinet."

And then he reminds me: the Friday of the Atlantic City trip is Veterans Day. Thad has Veterans Day off. He can take care of Blair. He can take Blair to music class. He can finally experience what it's like to be with her, alone, for more than a few hours in a row. So. I *should* want to go. I should jump up and down at the opportunity to get away for a night, even though that night will be my first night ever away from Blair. I *should*, also, care about that. My friend Kristen was so distraught about being away from *her* son for the first night ever that she broke down sobbing in the middle of a New Year's Eve party. A good mother is supposed to agonize about this landmark moment. A good mother is supposed to march into her boss's office and announce, firmly, perhaps with her arms folded in front of her chest, that it is not acceptable for the magazine to require her to be away from her child for a whole night. But I am not a good mother, because all I can think about is how awesome it will be to go to Atlantic City and get really, really drunk.

I start getting drunk at Red Square, my right hand balancing a martini glass filled with vodka, lime juice, dark rum, and sugar cane syrup that, when mixed together, is known here as a "Cuban Missile Crisis." Before I go to bed, I'll pump all that booze out of my boobs and flush it down the toilet—what the mommies and I call "pump and dump." I decide not to mention this term to Jessica.

"Your clothes are so coooool," Jessica says again.

"Um, thanks," someone says, and we all laugh like we're half-embarrassed, half-annoyed, except that I'm entirely pretending that I'm annoyed because, unbeknown to Jessica, I stopped at Stein Mart in Cherry Hill on my drive here and bought the long silver earrings and the short, fitted plum blazer I'm wearing and the black Kenneth Cole clutch that's wedged between me and the style editor and cost $80 on sale and is probably the nicest, most stylish thing I've purchased for myself since the $150 diaper bag with the cloth lining that now smells like banana. Jessica doesn't know that this whole getup is a disguise. I catch the eye of the waitress and order another Cuban Missile Crisis, then cross my legs and lean back, wondering why I'm not wondering if Thad had a hard time putting Blair to bed.

I drink somewhere between two and ten mojitos next door at Cube Libre where we have dinner, sitting at a very long table in the massive dining room designed to feel as if we're sitting on a street in Old Havana, with palm trees and brightly colored "houses" with clay roofs jutting over tables. There is lots of food—plantains and tuna ceviche and triangles of pressed cubano pork sandwiches. I take a short break from inhaling to run to the bar to call Thad to make sure everything is going okay. When I get back, I see that the tables in the main open area have been pushed to the side. The music stops for a second, then starts up again, a little louder, a little faster, as two dancers in yellow satin strut down the stairs from the second floor and begin to mambo. When they finish the dance, the guy crosses the room toward our table, holding out his hand to the style editor and the travel editor sitting at the far end. They shake their heads no. As he leans in closer, his arm out, bowing his head this time, I'm already out of my seat, walking so fast behind everyone's chairs that I might actually be sprinting.

"I'll dance with you," I announce, grabbing his hand, hearing claps and whistles from my table as he escorts me to the floor. Thad and I have taken ball-room classes, not to prepare for our wedding or anything, but because Thad is cool like that. We used to clear dance floors at weddings whenever a swing song came on, Thad so enthusiastic while he twisted me, again and again, for the pretzel turn that he'd squeeze my hand until I felt my finger bones scraping against each other. Yet I always kept smiling through the pain and the sweat, because I'd grown up on the stage. I was a performer. I'd been reared on the philosophy that the show must, always, go on.

This show, at Cube Libre, with the man in the yellow satin shirt that feels damp when I rest my left hand on his right shoulder, starts with a series of very basic cha-cha steps. I lift my shoulders, arching my back slightly, adjusting my torso into proper form.

"You've danced before," my partner says, my ears hearing a Spanish accent despite the fact that he doesn't have one.

"Yes, I have."

"You're good," he says, raising his eyebrow, grinning slightly before he tugs me in so close that his sweaty cheek brushes against mine for a few steps before he releases me in a roller coaster of spins and twirls that I would certainly have stumbled over if I'd had even a second to think about them—if I wasn't so mojitoed-up, and the lights weren't so bright, and I didn't feel like I was regressing, for one dance in a restaurant in a city I'd never been to before, to a time when this was what my life was. Out late. Drinking. Dancing. With no one at home to diaper.

Free.

Free to drink yet another mojito before a few of us stumble to the karaoke bar next door. Free to sing "Me and Bobby McGee" twice. Free to smoke four cigarettes. Free to head back to my room just before 2:00 AM, walking with the new executive editor, who is so drunk he gets off the elevator on the wrong floor. Free to pop four Advil in my mouth and chug them down with water from the tap, to leave my clothes all over the floor, to wear just my pajama top, to not pump, and then to hoard every single down pillow on the bed.

At 6:10 the next morning, my eyes explode open as if a fire alarm has started ringing. I can't pee fast enough, can't get dressed fast enough, not even taking advantage of the big shower and the bath products and the fact that I can leave my towels right there on the tile floor. I toss all my stuff into my suitcase. Only when I'm walking from the hotel to the parking lot down the street do I remember that there's a brunch I'm supposed to go to today where there will certainly be Mimosas. I don't stop. I don't care. I keep dragging my suitcase toward the garage, reaching in my new Kenneth Cole bag, which in the morning light looks very walk-of-shame-y dangling from my wrist, and pull out my cell phone to check the time—6:23. I start to walk faster, as if I'm late. I spot the parking sign I pulled under yesterday and drag myself there. I can't find a door. Before I consider any other options, I start trudging up the ramp, pulling my little black overnight suitcase, up one side, switch-backing, up the next side, switch-backing.

"Are you okay?" I hear someone say. I look up. I don't see anyone. I look behind me, no one.

"I'm fine," I yell out, waving to this phantom no one, in case someone actually is there and he is actually speaking to me. If he is there, I wonder what I must look like to him—hiking up the entrance ramp into a parking garage in high-heeled black boots, my hair tangled in a lopsided ponytail on the crown of my head, a thick uneven stripe of mascara under each eye.

I feel drops of sweat trailing down my spine as I switch back again, and again, my body now bent at a right angle to compensate for the grade of the ramp, my torso parallel to the floor. I don't know why, but I begin to jog, relieved on the next turn to spot the minivan in the first row of cars on what I suspect is the twenty-third floor. I peel out, my wheels screeching across the concrete, likely leaving a black scar of tire tracks that will stand as proof that I did this, I came here and spent the night and did what I was supposed to do. But this show is over now.

I realize, all of a sudden, why I'm rushing: there's nothing I want more right now than to get back home.

it's going
to suck

"Just invite any friendly-looking woman with a
baby in tow to come by for some coffee. Trust
me, they will be as eager for the companion-
ship, empathy and reassurance as you are."

—*The Girlfriend's Guide to*
Surviving the First Year of Motherhood

Thad is already thinking about sex. We're halfway
though our salads at a new bistro a few towns away
in Voorhees that the magazine publisher suggested I
go to because "it's so New York." It's our first date
since our wedding anniversary at the end of May.
Back then, Blair may have been miserable, but she
was portable. Now, she goes to bed in her crib exactly at 8:00, taking a bottle of formula instead of my
boob since I came home from that night in Atlantic
City and realized that, though I hadn't pumped in
more than twelve hours, there was nothing shaking
in there anyway and the nursing, finally, was done.

Now, if we want to go out, we need a sitter to come to our house.

Before Blair was born, I had all these grand plans about babysitters, about how I would call the high school where they teach a babysitting class and recruit some teenager in the neighborhood whom we'd keep on retainer every Saturday night for the rest of our lives. Then Blair was born and I realized that I was barely mature enough to keep my patience with Blair and that no teenager would be capable of shushing and bouncing her for hours and hours. I thought about calling the woman I met at the flower sale behind the grade school when I was out walking Blair during my maternity leave. She witnessed Blair cry for the entire eleven minutes I was there as I debated between hot pink and red impatiens, and she still leaned down so her smiling face was right in front of Blair's beet-red screaming one and said, "If you ever need a babysitter . . . I just love babies," before she wrote down her name and number on a crumpled pediatrician receipt I pulled out of the mesh basket under the stroller. Yet, when I physically picked up the phone to dial this woman's number, I couldn't press the buttons. *You have no idea who this woman is.* She could be a felon. She could be a sex offender. She could hand out her number to new, distracted, desperate moms all over Camden County, just waiting for one to call so she can kidnap the babe and flee to Poughkeepsie, where she'd assume a new name and raise the child as her own. In a trailer. Smoking pot with her before she sells her into the Russian prostitution trade.

Fortunately, my parents are in town, both retired as of last month, staying at a friend's vacant apartment in Center City for three weeks but spending most of their time in our house in the suburbs with Blair, which is where they are right now. I remember, years ago, when my mother told me that one of my cousins refused to let anyone but family members babysit her sons, I snorted, shaking my head, going off about how sheltered they were, how they had no lives, how their kids would grow up to be mama's boys who'd wear trench coats and fingerless black leather gloves and play Dungeons and Dragons. And, now, I've become them. Even though Blair doesn't cry like she used to. Even though we probably wouldn't leave until she was already in bed so the sitter would have nothing to do but watch HBO and eat our Doritos while she listens on the monitor to Blair moan when she rolls over every now and again. Or, maybe, I *want* to be my cousin. Maybe I want to have an excuse to stay home. Maybe I don't really want to do anything but lie on my own couch and eat my own Doritos and listen to my baby moan when she rolls over.

Or maybe I'm just afraid that a date with my husband will lead to the very comment he just made as he shoves butter into the crevice he knifed into the center of his multigrain roll.

"If you keep talking like that, you just might get lucky tonight."

"What?" I ask, not because I didn't hear him, but because I have no idea what I said to inspire him to say that. Last I recall, we were talking about how cute Blair's butt looks all fat with diaper, wiggling left and right when she crawls, which she just started doing two weeks ago, two days before Halloween. She hoisted herself up on her hands and knees, right after we got home from the pumpkin farm where Thad and I had frozen our own butts off as he dumped corn bits down long plastic tubes into the pens of llamas and goats and chickens with bulbous growths on their beaks. I tucked and retucked the fleece blanket tightly along Blair's body as she rode around in the stroller in a flimsy jean jacket since I hadn't bought a winter coat for her yet because all the ones I saw at the mall were too pink. When we got home, as I was popping the apple pie we bought into the oven, we watched as she teetered back and forth, lifted one knee forward, and crawled, officially crawled, across the rug to the spinning toy with the red suction cup on the end. And, ever since, that's been the only view we see of her, that wiggle butt crawling away from us.

But, apparently, Thad picked up something else in our first-course conversation, something that's got him fantasizing about rushing to the parking lot after dinner, before the movie, and folding down the stow-and-go rear seat in the minivan, tilting the stroller up on its end, and doing it. Here. In the parking lot of a strip mall, across from a Dollar Store, next to a Hair Cuttery.

It's not that I don't want to have sex in such close proximity to discount shopping. I just don't want to have sex.

In addition to appearing to be approximately the size of an economy car, my body feels like a car. Like a machine. Like it's been repurposed over the past eighteen months and now has an entirely different function. That area down there? That's for pushing out 6-pound, 14-ounce babies. Those things sticking out of my chest? Those are for feeding the aforementioned baby. And that is all. There's no gas left for anything else, certainly not for lying on my back on the gray carpet in the minivan, my newly repurposed flab spreading out underneath me like paste, me staring at the green stuffed snake twisted around the headrest above Blair's car seat, as Thad thrusts in the door that's now clearly marked "out," as in "the door through which small human beings arrive." Thad might as well just hump the gas line. The gas line probably feels sexier than I do, even though Thad constantly tells me how sexy he thinks I am, how sexy he thinks I look, how sexy he thinks my newly repurposed flab is. How can I explain to him that it doesn't matter what he thinks, especially when I know that it totally matters to *him* that I think *he's* sexy? And the way he thinks I best express these feelings is by having sex with him, which is why I've been enduring it about twice a month as if it's just another thing on my to-do list, as if it's work, adding the "good wife" ball to the "good mom" ball and the "good career gal" ball that I've been trying to juggle for the past nine months, mostly dropping them and watching as they roll down the street and tumble into the sewer.

"What do you think's going on over there?" I ask, hoping to distract him, pointing to the crowd gathered at the end of the bar.

"Birthday?" he suggests.

"Birthday," I say, noticing that everyone appears to be a few years younger than we are, on the other side of babies, some of them probably just recently married and having sex in motor vehicles all the time. I watch as a guy spins the ice in the bottom of his scotch and two women sneak outside for cigarettes, marching up and down to stay warm.

"That used to be us," I say.

"Yeah," Thad says. We both continue staring as if they're a primitive tribe and we're watching from a tour bus, trying to decipher their ways. "You know," he adds, still staring, "I'm kind of glad we're not them anymore."

"Yeah," I say.

• • •

Even I can't believe it has come to this—me, on the day after Thanksgiving, in my kitchen, in a face-off. With Thad's father.

I expected things to be different now. So did Thad. We hoped that, since there was a brand-new granddaughter in the picture, we wouldn't hear those same excuses Thad's parents had been using almost every time we invited them to visit us since we moved into our house two years ago—*there's no one to take care of the dogs; we can't drive in the dark; turkey season starts tomorrow.*

Thad's mother always wanted to come. In fact, she came on her own lots of times before Blair, and then drove down for a few days when Blair was still tiny to help out when Thad had to go to Boston for work. She jumped at the chance to have a relationship with this granddaughter since she's rarely seen her other one, Alexis, since Thad's brother, Terry, got divorced. More than anything, I think Thad's mom is grateful that we want to include her, or at least that's what I thought as she held Blair all those months ago, while

I slept and ran to Target and she cooked baked chicken and scalloped potatoes for dinner. I moaned to Thad for days about how weird it was going to be, having his mother there all day long. Just her. And me. Yet, at night, there we were, talking for hours on the couch about movies, about how much we hate Tom Cruise, watching *Dancing with the Stars*.

Thad's dad was a different story, but Thad was used to his not being around. His dad pretty much did his own thing, which meant hunting alone in the woods surrounding their house. And he was still doing that kind of thing, keeping to himself.

But then, something funny happened. Last year, Thad's dad retired from the glass factory where he'd worked in 120-degree heat every day for thirty-seven years and, for the first time Thad could remember, his dad started to tell his younger son that he loved him. And then, he came to the hospital when Blair was born, blotting his eyes with the hanky he pulled out of the back pocket of his jeans when he realized we'd named Blair after his father. And then, when I stopped at their house on the way to Erie for the Fourth of July, he posed Blair for photos on his black bearskin rug, as if the things he was most proud of in the world needed to be captured on film together. Thad felt as if he and his father had turned a corner, that his dad was suddenly taking an interest in him, his life, and his family.

I took this idea and ran with it—inviting the whole clan to our house for Thanksgiving, sending out invitations and everything. My parents took the train out to our house first thing in the morning to help me cook, the two of them bobbing and weaving around my kitchen as if it was their own, so familiar with it because they'd spent so much time here since Blair arrived. My mother was only half-kidding when she mailed us construction plans she'd cut out of *Country Living* magazine for turning our tiny one-car garage into an in-law suite.

Thad's family arrived a few hours later, his mom carrying a deep-dish apple pie, Terry lugging in tools to help Thad mount the vise in his basement workshop, Alexis looking more like a freshman in college than a freshman in high school. Terry made the gravy, my mom opened the chardonnay, and we all sat down at the dining room table that I'd decorated with red, orange, and gold mums.

"Let's all say something we're thankful for," I said to avoid the awkwardness of Thad having to improvise some kind of prayer, especially since the only reason he knew the "Our Father" was from playing football in high school.

All Alexis had to say was "I'm thankful that our family is together" to unleash the tears down Thad's mother's cheeks. I was shocked, not because his mother was so emotional, but because I looked down the table and caught Thad's dad dabbing the corners of his eyes. I almost laughed—not because it was funny, but because it caught me so off-guard. I would have been less surprised if the mums had started to cry. I had no idea Thad's father felt this way.

"We should do something tomorrow," Thad said as we lay in bed that night after his family went to sleep on blow-up mattresses in the basement and my parents took the train back to the city. "We should go somewhere as a family." I sensed the urgency in his voice, the need to prolong this breakthrough moment, this realization that his dad actually wanted to be here, with us. With Thad. With Blair. Because, even though Thad had long ago accepted the fact that he and his dad would never be close, he still wanted him to have a relationship with Blair. We both did. Especially now. Because now, we saw Blair differently than we did five months ago, when she was this screaming creature we felt embarrassed to ask other people to hold. Now, she was crawling. She was laughing. She was eating pureed turkey dinners out of jars. Now she was this little person. With a little personality. And we wanted to share her. We wanted her to be wrapped up in a family that was bigger than just Thad and me and these crazy old people from Erie. We wanted her to soak in her Grammy's love of reading. We wanted her cousin to teach her to kick a soccer ball and her uncle to show her how to fix cars. We wanted her Pappy to take her hiking in the woods and teach her how to make turkey calls and shoot bows and arrows.

"Let's go to the Constitution Center," I suggested to Thad in bed, certain everyone would have fun at this new museum in Philly. Plus, we would all be together. And that was the entire point.

The next morning, as I pulled the French toast casserole out of the oven, Thad announced the plan.

"That sounds cool," Thad's mom said without hesitation.

"Great," Thad said, smiling like he'd restored peace to the land. "We'll take off as soon as Blair wakes up from her nap, and then you guys can hit the road from there." Alexis nodded. Terry did, too. I heard Blair whimper on the monitor and rushed to her room to get her changed and dressed.

As I carried Blair into the kitchen, I overheard Thad's brother say, "I don't think this constitution thing is going to work out." Thad stood leaning against the stove, his arms crossed high in front of his chest.

"What?" I said, far too curtly.

"If we had known yesterday," Terry mumbled from the other side of the room. "If we'd been able to plan for it . . ."

"What needed to be planned?" I interrupted, desperately wishing Thad was someplace else, not hearing this. "It's on your way."

"Well, you don't understand that . . . "

"What I don't understand is why this family never does anything other than eat together," I said, handing Blair to Thad so I could put my hands on my hips. No one spoke.

"Listen." The word rose up from the corner of the family room, heavy and slow like the first lyric of a dirge. "We don't want to drive in the dark. It's just not going to happen." By the end of his sentence, Thad's father was standing directly in front of me, all 6 feet of him with his white hair and white beard and deep bass voice. I looked at Thad to see if he was slicing his hand across his throat to signal me to shut up. But he wasn't. He was looking at Blair, almost apologetically.

Seeing that expression on his face, it suddenly occurred to me that I hadn't been the only one struggling for the past nine months. It'd been hard for Thad, too, as he tried to figure out how to be a dad. It was no wonder he didn't think twice about going to the gym after work, or sticking around after his Ultimate Frisbee game to have a beer with the team. In his family, that's what fathers did.

But Thad had been doing so much more. Moments flashed in my mind like a slideshow: Thad flying a naked Blair around the house on his forearm; Thad walking in the door from work with a Target bag filled with little six-month dresses; Thad asleep on the couch with Blair asleep on his chest, her arm wrapped around his. Thad wasn't following in anyone's footsteps. He was making this all up as he went along, too. He deserved much more credit for that. And I'd barely been giving him any at all.

Which is why I'm not backing down. Why I am where no good wife should ever be. In a face-off. With her husband's father.

"It will not be dark when you get home," I counter.

"It will."

"Don't you want to spend time with your granddaughters?"

"She won't remember it anyway," Thad's father says, jutting his arm toward Blair.

The room goes quiet again. Even I don't know what to say. What *could* I say? What could anyone say to that?

She won't remember it anyway.

She will remember it?

Alexis will?

Thad will?

And, most importantly, you will?

You will.

She won't remember it anyway. The words ring in my head like an alarm.

•   •   •

The article was due yesterday. The writer knows that, because two months ago, when she turned in her article two weeks late, I had to reprimand her. I had to pull the "I'm the editor" card. This strategy is something I've been using a lot lately, now that Blair is mobile. Now that she's figured out how to use her thumb to pick things up, things as small as Cheerios. And pennies. And the little red berries that have just blossomed on the holly tree in our front yard. Which are surely poisonous. And would cause her to choke. Or go into anaphylactic shock. So I've figured out that yelling "no" works, at least to startle her enough to stop moving, scandalized by the shrieking noise coming out of the mouth of this woman. The woman who has just recently started to hum show tunes to her while feeding her a bottle in the glider rocker at night, always catching her eye, both of us holding the gaze, like we've gotten a little closer to figuring out who we are to each other. After I yell, I always explain—"I'm the mommy. And I said so," in a tone that's firm and commanding, yet so controlled that it likely sounded somewhat maniacal when I used it on the writer. "I'm the editor," I said, interrupting her excuses that were not only lame but inappropriate, which inspired her to slump down in the chair across from my desk, looking more like five years old than thirty. But it was effective. Or I thought it was effective.

But this morning, when I booted up my e-mail and did not see her name in my inbox, I sent her an e-mail with nothing but three question marks in the subject line.

Moments later, she wrote back: "Are you asking about the story? I can send it to you tomorrow."

I wrote back: "Are you kidding?"

She wrote back: "Look, I'm sorry I didn't send the story yesterday when I said I would. . . . What I don't need, frankly, is for you to make me feel like I'm being stupid."

I wonder if, maybe, she *is* five years old. I want to send her an e-mail that says, "What I don't need, frankly, are writers who don't do what they say they are going to do, what they are being paid to do. I don't have time for this. Do your job." I actually write the e-mail. I sit back and read it, admiring the structure, the way I echoed her own words. Then I select all the copy. And I hit "delete." The problem is, I need the story. I spin my chair around and look out my window, crafting a response in my head that will encourage her yet still reiterate the timeline and the fact that deadlines are set for reasons. I don't feel like an editor at all. I feel like a therapist. I start to ruminate on the hours I spend every day strategizing how to get what I need from writers, which comprises about 95 percent of my job, which I'll likely be doing until about 7:00 tonight, making it home in time to see Blair for maybe fifteen minutes before she goes to bed.

I need to tell Thad I'm going to be late. I forward the entire exchange between the writer and me to him, so he can read, firsthand, the ridiculous reason why I'm going to be late. Right before I hit "send," I add one more line to my message:

"Is this really my life?"

•   •   •

I'm running late for my lunchtime spinning class at the gym across the street from my office. I zip into the locker room, already unbuttoning my shirt, and grab a space on the wooden bench a few feet away from another woman who's getting dressed. I notice the bump. I inspect it for a minute to make sure that she is, in fact, pregnant. That she isn't just chubby. Or has big bones. Or an intestinal disorder that causes her stomach to distend halfway across the room. I notice the weird brown line bisecting her abdomen.

"How far along are you?" I ask.

"Thirty-one weeks."

"Wow . . . almost eight months," I say, nodding and then turning my head fast, certain that it's pasted with that cocky "been there, done that" expression that drove me crazy when I was pregnant, when women I'd passed on the elevator every day for four years without a single word looked down and saw my big belly and proceeded to share with me every detail of their emergency C-section or their child's first vomit. I thought, at the time, that nothing could be worse. Until I stopped being pregnant. Until the baby started crying. Until I realized I'd have gladly gone through labor and delivery ten times over, without drugs, in a straw hut in Africa, if I could've skipped the first five months of my child's life.

I felt the residue of that desperation again just this past Saturday, when I made my "Things to Do Before Christmas" list, which included the folder of work in my briefcase that I needed to deal with before Monday morning, and the baby gift I needed to buy for my cousin Becky, whose son was born more than a month ago, and the eggnog I needed to make to bring as hostess gifts to the three holiday parties we'd been invited to next weekend. As soon as Blair woke up at 7:15 AM, I was ready for her to go down for her morning nap. When she woke up from her morning nap, I was ready for her to go down for her afternoon one, just so I could get things done, so I could get on top of things, thinking, *Once I get back from the grocery store, I'll spend time with Blair.* On my way to check the toilet paper supply, I walked through the living room and saw Thad there, wearing his gray fleece as Blair sat upright on the brown couch next to the door while Thad zipped her into her corduroy jacket.

"I'm taking her to the playground," he said. "Wanna come?" This was a first—Blair's first trip to a playground, the one down the street at the elementary school where I was thrilled Blair would be going for kindergarten in four years because I'd heard kids there started learning French in first grade.

"I can't," I said. "I have too much to do." I walked into her room, digging around the closet until I found the turquoise skullcap someone gave us when she was born. I brought it out. "She needs a hat," I said.

"Come with us," Thad said, on the porch now, strapping Blair into her stroller. I jacked my head up, eye-dagger level to his face, expecting to blurt out something reprimanding like, "Do you think I *want* to make eggnog?" Instead, I turned on my heels, grabbed my winter coat off the hook behind the door, and snatched the house keys from the top of the piano.

"Let's go," I said. And off we went, pushing the stroller to the little playground two blocks away with the green slides and those rubber upside-down-helmet swings that Blair looked way too small to even fit into. But Thad lifted her out of the stroller. Thad carried her over. Thad threaded her feet through the holes and pushed. And Blair started squeaking. It was a sound I'd never heard her make before. And Blair opened her mouth in a wide smile, sucking in the fresh air, like she knew it was fresh and she knew it was air and she knew she needed a breath of it. I'd never seen her make that face before, either. And I wouldn't have seen it if I'd stayed at home, counting toilet paper rolls.

I realized there, at the playground, snapping photos of Thad sliding down a slide with Blair in his lap, that I'd finally crossed to the other side of something. I didn't know what it was, exactly, just that I'd been slowly inching over it during the past few months as Blair stopped nursing and started filling out and started looking vaguely human. As I felt oddly proud a few weekends ago, pushing her in a cart around the grocery store when the woman in the green visor behind the deli counter yelled across the produce section at us to see if Blair wanted a piece of cheese. As I figured out that working until 7:00 didn't mean anything except that I wouldn't see my child before she went to bed. As I started talking to other mothers more, with women at work or on the phone with out-of-town friends, new moms like me, whom I'd been avoiding for nine months so I wouldn't have to hear another story about how adorable Mia or Isabel or Noah was during those early months, how much they missed that precious time.

Now, though, on the other side of that precious time, buttressed by the conversations I'd had with the mommies, I didn't feel anymore that I had to pretend that time was so precious, that new motherhood was all sunshine and fulfillment and love. So I'd say something safe. I'd test the waters.

"It's been hard," I said to my friend Jenny in Center City when she called last month.

"It's fucking hard," she said, in return. And then there was Sascha, who told me she believed that if she let her four-month-old son "cry it out" every time he awoke in the night she would damage his soul. Jenn panicked because she was so tired she could barely raise her arms, but because it was her twin sons' "active and alert time," she called her sister to come over and wave something above their heads, certain that without it they would grow up to be stunted. Roxanne was so afraid she wasn't reading enough to her baby that she read *New Yorker* articles, out loud, to her daughter when she was four weeks old. Maureen was so desperate for adult contact after her baby was born that she'd stand in the driveway, holding her daughter, waiting for a neighbor to walk by and strike up a conversation. Sally remembered one weekday morning during her maternity leave, pulling on yet another sweatshirt caked with spit-up and yelling at her husband, "*You* get to go to work while I have to stay *here*." Even my mother, who never let on that my infancy was anything short of paradise for her, pulled out my baby book and showed me a series of photos of me in the bath, awkwardly glued on top of each other because, she said, "You had the most horrible diaper rash and I didn't want someone to look in this book one day and see it and know that I let that happen to you." And of course there was Nancy, who revealed to me last week, "I only liked Bella during those first months because my OBGYN put me on Zoloft."

I called my high school friend Krysia in Pittsburgh to find out when she was going to our hometown for Christmas. She asked me how it had been going.

"You know what?" I ventured. "It really sucked. It only just started not sucking."

"I know," she said.

"You *know?*"

"Yeah, we had a bitch of a time with Eli for, like, six months."

"Why didn't you tell me that before?"

"I did."

"No, you didn't."

"Yes, I did. At your baby shower, last Christmas. We were talking at lunch. I remember it so clearly. I said, 'Don't worry if you don't bond right away.'"

"Yeah?"

"Yeah. Well, it was a nightmare. All I wanted was to nurse him. And he wouldn't nurse. He hated it. I was so pissed off that no one could tell me how to fix the problem. And I gave up. For weeks, months, years, I kept thinking, 'If I'd tried this,' or 'I gave up too soon.' And, God, how I cried. . . . "

"Krysia," I said, slowly, almost pleading, "why didn't you tell me *that?*"

A half hour ago, right before I left the office for the gym, a message popped up in my e-mail inbox, from babycenter.com. I'd subscribed to the listserv early in my pregnancy, because the Website sent out weekly e-mails describing how the baby was developing. They've kept sending them, generally freaking me out every time I read a post about my child at eight months and three weeks, who is supposed to be pointing at things at this stage, though Blair isn't pointing at things, which makes me immediately picture her retiring in sixty-seven years from working as a cashier at a Sbarro at a turnpike rest stop. I almost deleted the message, until I read the subject line: "Twenty Things That Change When You Have a Baby."

Number 1: "You look at your baby in the mirror instead of yourself."

Number 2: "You finally stop to smell the roses because your baby is in your arms."

Number 4: "You're less self-involved and more self-motivated."

Number 5: "The sacrifices you thought you made to have a child no longer seem like sacrifices."

Number 6: "You respect your body . . . finally."

Number 13: "You think of your baby 234,836,178, 976 times a day. In fact, you're so busy with this that you forget everything else."

Number 17: "You become a morning person."

I wanted to scream. I did scream. "Are you friggin' kidding me!" I yelled, as I hammered down on the delete button as if the message were some kind of venomous bug. *This is exactly the problem,* I thought. *This is exactly why I spent six months feeling like a failure, why I spent seven months feeling so alone. Because the only thing that anyone ever tells you is that having a baby is going to be like this. It's going to be ROSES?* This should be illegal, all this mommy propaganda, all this la-la crap that's oozing out of every book and every article, that every aunt and every neighbor and every nurse at the OBGYN gushes forth like Sweet'n Low when you break the "I'm pregnant" news, that sets us up to have these expectations that motherhood is immediately, and forever after, bliss. And delight. And roses, for God's sake.

There were moments like that. Of course there were moments. But there was so much else going on, too, things that made me feel emotions that no one warned me I would feel. I was so paralyzed by it that there was no way I could talk about it. But the feelings kept raging and churning in my head, this battle over what I thought motherhood should be versus what I was really going through. How could I admit there was a difference? I had no choice but to get it right. I certainly couldn't let anyone think I was screwing up. But the face I put on—that things were fine—only made the battle worse. Only made me feel more alone.

And here I am at the gym, face-to-face with a woman who is eight months pregnant. She probably subscribes to babycenter.com, too. She probably got the same e-mail this morning. She probably believes that, in two months, she's going to miraculously become a morning person. And be happy about it.

"How are you feeling?" I ask her, pulling on the big loose sweatpants I wore to the gym when I was pregnant because they're just more comfortable than those skimpy bike shorts I used to wear.

"Pretty good," she says. "I'm starting to get tired."

"Yeah. That doesn't really go away. I have a nine-month-old at home and I'm still tired. Probably more tired than I ever was during the pregnancy."

I'm proud of myself. This is what I should do. Start a crusade. A movement. Mothers Who Break the Silence. Mothers Against Pretending They're Good Mothers. Mothers Who Didn't Like Their Babies Right Away. And here I am. Telling the truth. With a woman I don't even know. Who cares if I'm late for my class? She needs this. She deserves it.

"It's really hard. Just so you know. The beginning was harder than anyone ever told me it would be. If you feel lost or frustrated or guilty or anything, know that you're not the only one. Okay?"

"Wow. You really make it sound great," the pregnant woman says, sarcastically, squinching her eyebrows together. She turns away, then says, with her back to me, "Thanks a ton."

because it's
really ten months

"Like it or not, you are a family now.
You sink or swim together."

—*Your Baby and Child*

I have the distant memory of a moment.

It is my first memory, my first real, true memory that isn't sparked by any of the photos glued into my baby book or sealed under plastic in the blue-and-green-flowered photo album on the shelf in my parents' family room. In this memory, in this moment, I am a baby, I think around the same age Blair is right now. I'm in my crib, alone in my room on the second floor of my parents' split-level in Erie. I'm standing, holding myself steady with my hands clutching two of the bars of the wooden crib, staring at the door, which is cracked just enough that I can see a stripe of bright white light down the right side. I'm very excited, because my Grammy and Pappy are coming. They're driving from Pittsburgh, though I'm probably not aware that they're driving from Pittsburgh. But I know that I like the idea of Grammy and Pappy coming and maybe I know why—because I get to lie with them in the morning on the pull-out couch in the family room and because Pappy smells like soap and because they always bring their dog. I think I hear the front door open. I think I hear voices. I don't say anything. I just wait. Slowly, the door to my room glides open. The light shines in, but it doesn't hurt my eyes, so when I look down to the floor, I see the black-and-white Boston terrier, though I don't know that it's a Boston terrier or what a Boston terrier is. But I do know his name.

Mack.

I remember this moment as I climb up the steps to the second floor of my parents' house, far enough so that I can hear if any sounds are coming from that bedroom, that same room where Blair is napping right now, on the afternoon of Christmas Eve. We arrived last night and will be here for more than a week, since Thad and I both managed to take off from work for the same eleven days in a row. I haven't spent this much uninterrupted time with Blair since the last time I was in Erie, during maternity leave. Now, Blair is in the Pack 'n Play. To the left side, on the floor, is her white noise machine that we brought from home. The single bed next to the crib, my childhood bed with the trundle underneath and the springs that still squeak, has been transformed into a diaper-changing station, with a turquoise bath towel stretched across the plum bedspread in between a pack of size 1–2 Pampers Cruisers and a box of sensitive-skin wipes.

My other grandmother—the same one from the memory of that moment thirty-three years ago, except now we call her Gigi—usually sleeps in this bed when she's visiting, since Pappy died in 1984 and since the sleeper sofa was hauled to the church. And she's visiting now, from Pittsburgh, for Christmas, but she's relegated herself to the couch in the family room, despite our protests that an eighty-eight-year-old woman, with lung cancer no less, should not sleep on a couch. We could set up Blair's Pack 'n Play in the top-floor bedroom where Thad and I always sleep, in the two Dick Van Dyke–esque twin beds jutting out from opposite walls. Or Gigi could sleep on one of the Dick Van Dykes and Thad could sleep on the couch. But my grandmother insisted she liked the couch. My mother explained that Gigi can sleep "anywhere" and that, once she falls asleep, "she doesn't even move until morning." What no one said, but what they all were thinking, was that all things, now and forever, shall defer to Blair and Blair's needs and Blair's comfort and Blair's personal happiness.

"I guess Blair's 'The Polish Princess' now," my dad yells from the kitchen, as I creep backward down the stairs, stripping me of the title he bestowed on me as a kid. I'm sure, if I'd been listening to him a little more closely, I would feel a tad bit melancholy that I no longer hold the center of attention in this house where, even now with a child of my own, I still regress to the child I was when I lived here, lying on the couch in front of the TV, letting my mom bring me the beaters with chocolate chip cookie dough on them, letting my dad wake me up in the morning instead of using the alarm, as if I haven't been living on my own, cooking my own meals, hanging up my own coats in my own closet, for almost half my life.

But I'm far too preoccupied with the moment I just remembered as I crawled up the steps that I can't rightfully mourn the passing of the princess torch, not with my mind churning the way it is, so fast that I sit down on the couch in the living room, hoping the stable position will force my thoughts to settle out. I wish Thad were here, not at the gym a few blocks away, so I could puzzle this out with him, so I could get his take.

My first memory takes place when I'm around ten months old.

I don't remember anything that happened before.

Maybe this means Blair won't remember anything either.

Maybe Blair won't remember crying, being trapped in swaddles, needles in her heels for the bilirubin tests, falling out of her swing, starving, Thad and me fighting, me talking to myself about how much I hate this, about how I don't know what to do, about how I don't know if I can handle any more, about how I'm not sure if I love her.

Maybe Blair won't remember these second nine months at all.

Last night, a few hours after we pulled into the driveway, my friend Stacy stopped by. She'd flown into Erie from Arizona, where she'd been living since she stopped to meet Blair nine months ago, working with birds of prey on the Hopi Indian reservation. Her dad was in the hospital. He'd been sick for years, with serious diabetes and heart issues, but now he seemed to be getting worse, to the point at which the doctors she spoke to on the phone were discussing his prognosis in terms of weeks, not months. Even so, she carried a bag of presents, not even taking her coat off before she handed one to me.

"Open it," she instructed.

"Why don't you get a glass of wine or something. . . . "

"Open it," she said again, more insistently this time, sitting down directly in front of me on the living room floor.

I unwrapped the package. Inside were a pair of maracas, one turquoise and the other yellow, with feathers sticking out of the top of each.

"My friend made these for you. They're supposed to help calm babies, to stop babies from crying. That's why the Hopis use them. To calm their babies."

She sat up very straight, looking very pleased, as if she had just solved every problem I'd ever had in my entire life.

I smiled back, hoping she couldn't tell that I was thoroughly confused. I knew she hadn't seen Blair in nine months and hadn't yet seen her that night, since Thad was upstairs in the bedroom changing her into her pajamas. But I didn't understand. Was she thinking I'd use these on Blair? Did she think that Blair was still fussing, still crying, still the same child she was when Stacy first met her, the one with the bulging eyes that I can only remember when I look at the photos we took back then?

Apparently, she did think that. Of course she did. Of course Stacy thought Blair would still be the baby she was. Of course she didn't know Blair would evolve and grow. *I* didn't know. I had no idea we'd ever be here, on this day, and that Blair would be the baby she'd become, sitting up and smiling and proudly tearing the paper off presents all by herself and saying "dada" since last month and "mama," which happened for the first time last week. I couldn't fathom these things as even possibilities back when I was shuffling around the house with this Martian sucking on my boob as I lunged, up and down, up and down, to distract her from emitting those cries I didn't understand, couldn't soothe, wanted to run away from. And now. Now I can barely remember those moments. When I think of them, I see the scenes play behind my eyes like a movie, like I'm an actress and Blair's an actress, and we're playing roles.

Yes, Blair has changed. But the real change has happened in me. And I can't point to the day when it happened, or the second when I realized that things were different, or the morning I woke up and felt like everything was going to be okay. There wasn't a switch that flipped. I always expected a switch to flip. There was no switch. There is no switch. There is no maternal gene that clicks on the moment the delivery room nurse places the baby on your chest. I had to learn how to be a mother.

Certainly, it's more than learning the mechanics of changing diapers and securing car seats in shopping carts and sensing when Thad is at his wit's end with her squirming on the changing table and needs me to swoop in with a puppet on my hand. It's more than learning how to manage the crying, which rarely happens now, and then, later, the tango in the morning to get us both dressed and fed and Blair's lunch packed before I take her to Jane's and I drive to the train station. And then, even later—because there's always something, there's always going to be something—the game of chicken I play with myself in the middle of the night if she wakes up and starts to cry and I lie in bed, wide awake, waiting to see if she cries long enough or hard enough or strangely enough for my internal alarm to ring and propel me down the hall and into her room, where I rub her back and explain, "It's still sleepy time."

It's learning that I'm not an editor by day and a mother by night. I'm not divided into befores and afters, into olds and news. I'm both. And I've had to learn that that's okay. I appreciate the way the new me reads a posting on babycenter.com in the middle of my workday about how reading to children is the most important part of their development, and then the old me takes over and forwards the posting to Thad, insisting he agree to read at least one book a day to Blair and promising to do the same myself. Then that night, the new me sits on the floor in the family room with Blair in my lap and *Guess How Much I Love You?* in my hands, which she pushes away—and the old me ruminates there on the floor about how she'll never get into college, especially since, last Friday, Joan told all of us that every time Genni passes their Christmas tree she says, "Chee." Which was why I dispatched Thad to the Home Depot the moment he walked in the door that night to buy a Fraser fir that I decorated instantly, even though we'd be home to look at it for only seven days. Then I picked up Blair and held her in front of it and said, probably 437 times, "Tree. Tree. Can you say 'tree'?"

The next morning, I hear Blair whimper on the monitor. I look at the clock. It is 6:52 AM, Christmas morning. Twenty minutes pass, twenty minutes of on-and-off crying, which is how she wakes up in the morning, slow and fighting all the way. And it has been twenty minutes of me lying there, in the Dick Van Dyke by the window, waiting for Thad to get up. I know he hears her. I know he woke up, even though he has not moved in the past twenty minutes, playing dead so that I will do what I always do, what I've done every Saturday and Sunday morning since she's been sleeping through the night: I'll either get up myself, or I'll ask him to get up. And today, just like every Saturday and Sunday, I'm waiting, waiting for him to take charge, waiting for him to give me a break, to get up himself. *He'd better be dead*, I think. I picture myself creeping over to his bed and pouring the glass of water on his nightstand on his neck. Or climbing up so my feet are squatting on either side of his waist before I start jumping up and down. Or poking him in the abdomen, right on his bladder, and yelling in his ear, "I know you hear her! And you wonder why you aren't getting as much sex as you used too? Helllllllooooo!"

I wait another minute. Thad still doesn't move.

I throw off the comforter, pull on my slippers, and wonder why I don't slam the door behind me. And then I remember why, an hour or so later, when everyone's awake, including Thad, whom I woke up after changing Blair's drenched morning diaper, and who is now wearing the Santa Claus hat my mother bought him as part of his New Dad Prep Kit. As my parents and grandmother meander downstairs to begin opening gifts, I pour my second cup of coffee and walk, slowly, to the top of the steps. I look down and I see Thad, in the hat, holding Blair, in her Christmas jammies, a red one-piece with little white snowmen on it. They're standing in front of the tree.

"Tree," he says. "Can you say 'tree'?"

•　　•　　•

I get up for my first day back to work on January 3, earlier than I usually do. I want to take my shower before Blair wakes up. That's my New Year's resolution: to take my shower and get dressed before she wakes up so we have a few minutes to play before I drop her at Miss Jane's and rush to the train station. So I have time to spend with her instead of locking her in the bathroom with me while I shower, singing *Open and Shut Them* from her music class over and over until she starts to cry and I begin the game of peek-a-boo, sliding open the shower doors one at a time, left and then right, hoping she'll start to anticipate which will be next, then handing her a damp washcloth to chew on while I blow-dry my hair.

As I shave my legs in the shower this morning, I wonder if I made a mistake, if my clock wasn't set right when I fell into bed last night, because it doesn't feel like it's 6:30. It feels like it might be closer to 3:00, what with the way my fingers haven't started functioning properly and I haven't yet opened my eyes. I decide that I'm just tired because the past eleven days have been tiring. Being with Blair all day, every day, entertaining her all day, every day, has been tiring. I'm not used to it. Neither is Thad. Even last night, I watched the clock as she hammered her new rainbow xylophone with the wrong side of the red mallet. It was 7:26 PM. Then 7:32. Then 7:42, when she crawled over to the fridge while Thad was pulling out a bottle of Yuengling, hoisting herself up so she was standing, almost on her tiptoes, reaching out to grab the skinny bottle of Tabasco. She'd learned about the fridge last week at Nana and Poppy's. She loved the fridge. 7:46. Fourteen more minutes until bedtime.

I convinced myself last night that this clock watching was the past eleven days just catching up with me, and with Thad, who I spotted glancing at the clock as often as I was. But that wasn't true. That was how it was every night. Waiting for her bedtime so we could have *our* time, which mainly consisted of watching TV, but didn't have one thing to do with a single primary-colored item that played a song. Every night, I always heard my mother's voice in my head: "Oh, we just loved that time of night with you. You'd be playing so well, we'd just let you stay up as long as we could. We didn't want you to go to bed." And, every night, I would decide that there was something terribly wrong with me that I spent most of my evenings with Blair waiting for her to go to sleep. I wondered if there would ever be a time when I wouldn't think I was doing something wrong, when I wouldn't think I was being a bad mother. Maybe that's what being a mother was. Just then, I remembered an e-mail I found from a coworker as I was weeding out my inbox before the holiday. She'd sent it to me during my maternity leave, though I can't recall reading it then: "Some people, their kids ground them. Other people, their kids shake them up. I'm afraid you and I are doomed to be shaken up. But that's what we get for being so sure we're on top of things all the time."

This morning, while Thad feeds Blair oatmeal, I pack her lunch bag, half watching the *Today* show. Usually Thad would be gone by now. But this morning he's taking his time. He's not even really watching the TV as he scrapes rogue blotches of mixed grains from the corners of Blair's mouth. Thad helps me wiggle Blair into her corduroy coat, and I nestle the green skullcap on her head before I pull up her hood. He straps her into the car carrier and lugs it to the minivan, as I hit the button on the key chain to make the electronic door slide open, all without speaking, without needing to confer because it's all just so normal now, so regular, like she's always been here, and we've always driven her around the corner to Jane's. I climb into the front seat of the van. Thad gets into his Jetta and pulls away before I back out of the driveway. I'm halfway down the street before I remember it, stopping the van and cocking the gear into reverse, as I weave backward until I'm parked along the curb right in front of our door. I grab the keys out of the ignition, think about pulling Blair out and bringing her in with me, then think again. *This will only take a second. I'm a bad mom for leaving her here. But this will, literally, only take a second.*

"I'll be right back, kiddo," I say, flipping the radio to CD mode and listening to the soundtrack from her music class blast, mid-song, from the speakers. I run up the front steps, fight the lock that's a tiny bit frozen, jog through the porch, through the door to the living room, and grab the photo sitting upright on the piano just by the coat rack. It's the photo my mother gave me for Christmas. She gave one to both Thad and me, in identical silver square frames. It's a photo of Blair, crawling toward the camera, dressed in the purple hooded velour sweat suit her "Aunt" Stacy sent her from Arizona last fall. Her eyebrows are raised and her eyes are smiling even more than her mouth, with her two little bottom teeth peeking over her bottom lip. She looks like she's going somewhere. She's moving forward. Moving on.

When I get back into the van I tuck the photo into my black leather work bag. I know exactly where I'm going to put it in my office—on the credenza where I can see it from my desk, and where anyone else who walks by, anyone who sits down in one of my chairs, can see it, too. I spin around the corner to Jane's and pull up alongside the curb.

"Baby Blair! Baby Blair!" Samantha yells in her squeaky two-year-old voice, running over to the door at Jane's as Blair and I barrel through.

"We missed you, sweetie," Jane says, helping me unhook Blair from the car seat. I put Blair's lunch bag on Jane's dining room table.

"Bye, Blair," I say. "Have fun," I say. "I love you."

I crawl back in the minivan but can't put the gear into drive. I don't want to leave. I consider it: going back in, grabbing Blair's coat and driving home, opening her toy box and handing her the purple doll she got for Christmas, and then dialing my boss on my cell phone, telling him that I won't be coming in anymore.

I don't, though. I can't. That's not the mother I am. I pull away. But I don't make it to the end of the block before tears are running down my face.

This time, for real.

acknowledgments

If I hadn't been given the opportunity to write this book, I suspect the story would have exploded out of the top of my head so, I must first thank my agent Larry Weissman for rescuing me from the mess of that and for recognizing the value in this idea and fighting hard for it, even though he and his wife, Sascha, swear the second nine months with their kids, Jack and Viv, were nothing but bliss. The crew at Da Capo could not have been more dedicated, especially Kate Burke and my editor Wendy Holt, who not only knew exactly when to push me to birth this thing but also advised me many times not to "worry so much," which is something I generally need to be reminded of. Thanks to Tom McGrath for making me write some of this down (while I was still on maternity leave, no less) for *Women's Health*, and Larry Platt for making me dig into it again for *Philadelphia* magazine under the wing of my editor Bob Huber who, as always, forced me to delve deeper than I thought I was capable of, even more so when he graciously read the first draft of this book, along with Tina Hay, Chas Brua, Krysia Vila-Roger, and Priscilla Baker (who should edit books for a

263

living). Special thanks to my second sets of eyes, Lynne Smyers and Michael McCormick, my consigliere Sasha Issenberg, and my dear friend April White who kept me sane throughout this entire process. This book wouldn't be what it is without the brave people in it, who all let me use their real names and tell their real stories (medals of courage go to Bella's daddy, Dave, and to my father-in-law, who, last time he visited, blew bubbles with Blair all morning long). The mommies—especially Jenn, Joan, and Nancy—pretty much saved my life during the second nine months and also last week, as did the incredible mothers who've been with me from the beginning, Essie Shields, Dorothy Glembocki (the mother of the sweetest, kindest, most patient father on the planet), and, above all, my own mom, Judy Glembocki—I can only hope I'm half as good at this as she's been. It is a rare man who would encourage his wife to document the dark details of their most trying hours, but I've always known that Thad is a rare man, and the only one I'd want by my side as we forge ahead through this parenting jungle. Drew has no idea how much she helped me write this book, from the inside out—when she can finally read it, she'll be so relieved she was born second, precisely four hours and seventeen minutes after I turned in the final manuscript. And, finally, I'm most grateful for Blair, and to Blair, for teaching me that there should always be time to run your fingers through the sand.